Be the best you can be

This book is a significant resource for people wanting to review their life and discover new directions. Neil's fresh, engaging style and unique framing help you to explore at your own pace. The models enable you to understand your thoughts and feelings and plan a way ahead. Neil possesses a restless intellect and a powerful drive to seek to share his learning. Using this book has the possibility to change your life!

Alison Cansdale, Therapeutic Life Coach,
Pastoral Supervisor, Lecturer

I have been inspired, motivated, and encouraged to be reflective through Neil's work. He makes it easy to review where you have come from, your achievements and where you are going next. I plan to continue my coaching journey with Neil supporting me all the way!

Deborah Gibbon, Headteacher, Jenny
Hammond School

Neil has coached me from my first steps in executive leadership to becoming a systems leader. He has helped me to think, make sense of the world and reframe the challenges on this bumpy journey through life and work. He is incredibly well read and has the ability to bring wisdom and practical examples to help unlock next steps. This book opens up the tools and techniques to an even wider audience – what a great thing!'

James Heale, THEP Director of Leader-
ship and Development & Founder, Fly-
wheel Learning Ltd

I have lost count of the senior leaders and teachers who have benefited from Neil's experience and passion. He is approachable, engaging, warm, knowledgeable, and funny. His teaching is well paced, involving a balance of theory, practice, and reflection. With Neil's guidance, coaching becomes a way of life that enables us to reach our full potential. Just amazing!

Marie-Anne Leregle, West London
Alliance Lead

Neil's coaching has had a profound impact on my role and my life. His deep expertise and compassionate approach have guided me to look at problems through multiple lenses. This has truly empowered me. This book is a testament to his ability to guide readers toward a more purposeful and intentional way of living. I cannot recommend it enough!

Navroop Mehat, Headteacher, Wexham Court School

I have worked with Neil for 25 years in medical education. He is highly professional, extremely knowledgeable, the very best of communicators and a passionate coach. He exemplifies 'Living a Conscious Lifestyle'. Whatever he writes is really worth reading!

Dr Brynmor Neal
MB BS FRCGP,D.Obst RCOG

Neil models an intentional and conscious approach to living. Over the pages of this book, you will discover the thoughtful, skilful, and structured coaching that I have found invaluable in navigating life and its many challenges.

Paul Thomas, Lead Pastor, King's Church Amersham

Wisdom, integrity, and humanity underpin all of Neil's work, making him a truly inspirational coach. He excels at creating a reflective environment. In this thought provoking, practical book, he supports the reader in working towards their preferred future. Prepare to feel empowered!

Tracy Warner, Multi Academy Trust Executive Principal

A phenomenal coach - Insightful, challenging, reassuring. Over and over, Neil has asked the 'inch-perfect' question that has enabled me to find my personal answers. He is honorable, generous and genuine.

Richard Yates, Principal, West Drayton Academy

LIVING
A
CONSCIOUS
LIFESTYLE

How to be the best you can be

LIVING
A
CONSCIOUS
LIFESTYLE

How to be the best you can be

Dr Neil Suggett CBE

neilsuggett.com

To Judith

My best friend, life-long encourager, and wife

With thanks to:

My interviewees for their wisdom and openness

Stephen McClelland — my friend and publisher
who made this book a reality

Dr Neil Suggett CBE

Dr Neil Suggett is an acknowledged international authority on coaching and leadership development and a frequent speaker at major conferences.

Neil has worked as a teacher, head teacher, inspector and leadership coach. He has been a researcher at the National College, a Visiting Fellow at the Institute of Education and a Visiting Lecturer at Loughborough University and Brunel University. As one of the first National Leaders of Education, he has worked extensively in people development and school improvement.

He has coached on five continents and is very passionate about the power of coaching to transform both individuals and organizations everywhere. His current 'Platinum Group' of coaching clients include senior leaders in all phases of education and senior church leaders.

In 2010, Neil was awarded the CBE in recognition of his services to education at home and abroad. In 2016, he was also honoured by The Royal College of General Practitioners in recognition of his services to medical education.

He now enjoys working as a leadership coach, coach trainer and writer. Currently, he is engaged in designing and delivering coach development programmes in a variety of contexts — locally, nationally and internationally. Most importantly, he is an ardent life-long learner committed to 'living a conscious lifestyle'.

Contents

Introduction

A life well lived is a precious gift

Of hope and strength and grace,

From someone who has made our world

A brighter, better place

It's filled with moments, sweet and sad

With smiles and sometimes tears,

With friendships formed and good times shared

And laughter through the years.

A life well lived is a legacy

Of joy and pride and pleasure,

A living, lasting memory

Our grateful hearts will treasure (Author Unknown)

This book has been a long time in the making. It is written in the hope of encouraging you (and myself) to pause, reflect and consider a lifestyle that is by design rather than by default. Socrates suggested that "The unexamined life is not worth living."[1] This is an extreme view, but I have some empathy with the sentiment. Let me pose the question that arises from this statement. 'How much time have you invested in reviewing your lifestyle and making conscious decisions about navigating the joys and challenges of your existence?'

Confucius taught that "By three methods we may learn wisdom: by reflection, which is the noblest; by imitation, which is the easiest; and third by experience, which is the bitterest."[2] *Living a Conscious Lifestyle* requires a willingness to reflect, learn and plan the future.

The five sections of the book are arranged in the following order:

Looking back - a retrospective review of your unique history

Looking forward – a prospective view of your future life

Looking outwards – a personal view of your outer world

Looking inwards – an introspective view of your inner world

Looking at the NOW – the place where these four perspectives collide

This two-dimensional cross in Figure 1 is a visual representation of the five sections. The horizontal axis represents time – your past and your future. The vertical axis represents your perspective – looking outwards and looking inwards. The NOW is where these four perspectives cohere, the nexus of the views from these four standpoints. The NOW might not be in the middle of the diagram because your age and stage will define where you are on the horizontal access. Similarly, your NOW might not be in the centre of the vertical axis depending on your interest and preferences for looking outwards or inwards. Both axes are significant in focusing on the NOW. They each hold the other in balance.

Lao Tzu believed that "Knowing others is wisdom; knowing yourself is enlightenment."[3] A life well lived should be both a worthy aspiration and a daily reality. It could happen by chance, a combination of luck and serendipity, or it could happen by design. I prefer the second alternative. *Living a Conscious Lifestyle* provides an opportunity for you to reflect in a systematic way on your history, your future aspirations, the nature of your outer world and the quality

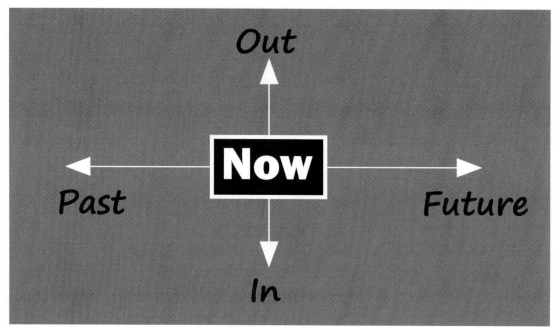

Figure 1 NOW seize the day

of your inner thinking. The underlying imperative of the book is *carpe diem* – NOW seize the day.

Each of the five chapters of the book is structured in a similar way:

It will begin with explanatory text highlighting the golden threads of the section, supported by references from the wider literature. The themes identified are drawn from a combination of my own thinking and the recurring themes emerging from a range of lifestyle interviews conducted over the last five years. Thirty people have given their time and energy to answer my questions. Direct quotes from these interviews are presented in italics at appropriate points in the text. These testimonies reflect the lived and current reality of the individual interviewees and are presented unalloyed, without commentary. The quotes are not referenced to a particular interviewee to maintain confidentiality.

Each chapter will be concluded with practical exercises to deepen your reflection and support your planning in this area. This is the place where you design your future lifestyle.

This book has been shaped by my own experience, the reading I have undertaken, and the interviews I have conducted. As a baby boomer, I am the product of a perspective that reflects my age and lived experience. Ken Wilber[4] believes that 'boomer weaknesses' include an unusual dose of self-absorption and narcissism — you will have to judge for yourself! My aspiration is to integrate my own experience and learning in a way that provides a starting point for your own reflection, learning and future planning.

The books that have shaped my thinking are identified at various points in the text. I have not set out to undertake a comprehensive review of the lifestyle planning literature. Quite the contrary, serendipity and accidental collisions have led me from one book to another. Some books have challenged my thinking, some have underscored what I already thought, and some have been a major disappointment!

The people I have interviewed for this book have been a source of inspiration. They are by no means a representative cross-section of the population, but they all share one common characteristic – they are alive and living their own idiosyncratic lifestyle. As Margaret Mead opined, "Always remember that you are absolutely unique, just like everyone else".[5] I am very grateful for their time and willingness to answer my questions. I had not realised the depth of self-revelation and openness people would be prepared to embrace, although I am very grateful that it was so!

The questions I posed were based around the five sections outlined above. The first interview was conducted in November 2017 and the final one in November 2022 – five years. This represents a long gestation period, and the questions were modified over that period. The ten questions in the final interview schedule are set out below.

Living a Conscious Lifestyle Questions

PAST

How has your history shaped your life?

What experiences have had the biggest impact on you?

FUTURE

What 'purpose' drives and inspires you?

What future possibilities excite you?

OUTWARDS

How would you describe your prevailing mindset?

Where are the boundaries of your comfort zone?

INWARDS

How do you manage reflection as a development activity?

How do you respond to feedback and criticism?

NOW

How do you manage your health (physical, mental, and spiritual)?

How would you like to shift the balance of your life in terms of 'more of' and 'less of'?

I gave my interviewees the choice of having the questions beforehand or responding spontaneously on the day. There are arguments for both approaches and the richness of the responses indicated that they both worked well. Perhaps the choice the interviewees made reflected their approach to life? Their answers revealed some of their hopes and fears and provided a small window into their approach to conscious and unconscious lifestyle planning.

I reviewed each interview at some length and endeavoured to identify the recurring themes or 'golden threads' that were emerging. This could be described as an ethnographic approach, an attempt to understand the reality of the respondent. Over time some very clear themes emerged, and these will be elaborated in the five chapters. Inevitably the ethnographer exercises some editorial power and there is always the possibility of manifesting elements of the self-fulfilling prophecy and personal preference.

Let me be crystal clear: I have no desire to define what you, the reader, should think. My motivation for writing this book is to provide you with a springboard for your own lifestyle planning. My aspiration is to supply some starting points and tools to scaffold your thinking. I love hearing about other people's lives and the interview material suggests some fruitful themes. The tools are included to provide some practical signposts to get you started. Use the ones that pique your interest.

I have structured the book around the two-dimensional cross and I suggest you work through the sections in the order I have presented them. Of course, this approach is not mandatory, you may choose to start with the section that most captures your interest. My strong recommendation is that you start a new learning journal to record your reflections and new thinking as you work through the material. Pace your learning in the way that works best for you. Your insights may be for your eyes only or you may choose to seek the feedback and wisdom of others. The choice is yours!

Whatever your approach, I urge you to record your thinking in a systematic and progressive way. Start your learning journal the day you start reading the book. This might be a leather-bound book, a loose-leaf folder or a document or your iPad or phone – it does not matter. Date each entry and watch your life-style design take shape.

Let's get started with the first exercise. Record your answers to the ten questions I posed to my interviewees – you might like to reflect for a few days or simply write down the first thoughts that come into your head. Note your thoughts and see where your answers lead. Reflect on these answers and come back to them when you have finished working through the book. As the saying goes, 'A journey of a thousand miles starts with a first step.'[6]

Now is time to take the first step.

Exercise 1: Living a Conscious Lifestyle Questions

PAST
How has your history shaped your life?
What experiences have had the biggest impact on you?

FUTURE
What 'purpose' drives and inspires you?
What future possibilities excite you?

OUTWARDS
How would you describe your prevailing mindset?
Where are the boundaries of your comfort zone?

INWARDS
How do you manage reflection as a development activity?
How do you respond to feedback and criticism?

NOW
How do you manage your health (physical, mental, and spiritual)?
How would you like to shift the balance of your life in terms of 'more of' and 'less of'?

Bibliography

1. Socrates - the-philosophy.com, 2. Confucius – brainyquote.com, 3. Lao Tzu – brainyquote.com, 4. Wilbur, K (2000) A Theory of Everything, 5. Margaret Mead – lifehack.org, 6. A Proverb – phrases.org.uk

The past

A reflection on your unique history

R D Laing[1] famously asserted that "Our behaviour is a function of our experience." This is not a determinist mantra, rather it is an observation of the human condition. Our history shapes the way we see the world. We look at life through the spectacles of our accumulated experience. We may choose to have an eye test and change the prescription on our spectacles, but our history exerts a powerful influence on the way we frame current reality. This may be a largely unconscious process and we are unaware of the gravitational pull of our past.

In this first chapter, I plan to share reflections on my own history and some of the recurring themes from the interviews I have conducted. Please read this material with a generous frame of mind and use the themes as a way of reconnecting with your own history. Saint Paul asserts in 1 Corinthians 13:12 "For now we see through a glass darkly."[2] Our memories may be distorted and fragmentary, but the experiences have undoubtedly shaped us. Libraries full of psychological tomes have been written on child and adult development and this introduction to 'your unique history' is not intended to be either comprehensive or exhaustive. It is designed as a thought starter to stimulate reflections on your own life.

What is your earliest memory? John Bowlby[3] suggested that the first three years have a critical influence on the rest of our lives. This is a period of rapid growth when we find out about the world and our place in it. It is a phase characterised by the acquisition of language and the ability to frame questions. Young children exhaust the people around them, (especially their grandparents), with an endless string of 'why' questions. This is a helpful approach to carry into later life. Indeed, Edgar Schein believes "Questions are taken for granted rather than given a starring role in the human drama. Yet all my teaching and consulting experience has taught me that what builds a relationship, what solves problems, what moves things forward is asking the right questions."[4] Bruce Lipton, the former medical school professor, and research scientist, suggests in his ground-breaking work in the field of New Biology that our underlying beliefs are firmly established in the first six years of life.[5] He further suggests in his work on epigenetics, that many of them may be limiting beliefs!

Most children grow up in a family. John Cleese authored a book *Families and how to survive them*[6] and this rather sardonic title captures an essential truth about the nature of early socialisation. Attitudes and values are formed in the crucible of family life. No two families are the same and some young children grow up outside a family setting. Families come in a variety of shapes and sizes – the permutations are endless. Your birth position in the family may also be an influence on how you are treated and how you see yourself.

History Reflection Point 1 – Parenting

What has been the impact of your parents on your life?

It is a truism that you do not get to choose your parents. You are born into an existing family or outside one. The choices your parents make about their lives will impact yours in all sorts of ways. Life deals you a hand of cards and when you are mature enough to have agency, you decide how to play them.

Examine the hand you have been dealt & make the most of it.

Most of my interviewees reflected on the impact of their parents or care-givers.

They are critical reality defining figures in your early life and often continue to exert a surprisingly lasting influence in your later life. I have chosen to focus on four recurring themes.

>> The presence or absence of parental love.

>> The socio-economic circumstances of the family.

>> The expectations that were stated and unstated.

>> The educational experience that was chosen.

The significance of parental love

"There is only one happiness in this life, to love and be loved."[7] George Sand may be highlighting an eternal truth in this statement, or he may be over exaggerating the power of love. Several interviewees referred to their experience of the unconditional love of their parents, although it was taken-for-granted in their childhood. Their assumption was that it was a universal experience. Others referred to the perceived lack of love in their upbringing and expressed enduring regret about this experience.

> My parents loved me unconditionally and made significant sacrifices to facilitate my development

> Gravity in the physical world integrates, love is emotional gravity in life.

> I had a relatively happy childhood, although my father showed no outward affection.

> My parents never gave a s**t about family and saw children as an inconvenience.

Four interviewees and four very different experiences. Eleanor Mills provided her own conclusions on the impact of love in a newspaper article on 13th August 2021. "I was bred to believe that happiness lay in achievement and status. Now I know it comes from feeling loved unconditionally, from being known for your essential self."[8] The personal life-line exercise later in this chapter provides an opportunity to reflect on your own history.

The socio-economic circumstances of the family

> You do not choose where you land! I was fortunate to be born into a middle-class family, in a first world country.

Babies are born into very different situations. As a baby, you have no control over 'where you land' or who your primary care givers are. My sample of interviewees was never intended to be a cross-section of the population and was skewed to well-educated, middle-class people. Some of the interviewees identified their parents as working class, without defining that designation further. Crude measures of socio-economic circumstances were alluded to in passing and they included wealth, housing, level of education and parental occupations. Abundance and scarcity provide opposite ends of an invisible continuum, or at least a child's dawning perception of their own circumstances.

> I was born into a nice family and was privately educated.

> I was increasingly aware of material scarcity.

> You don't need a lot of money or things to be happy, it is about making the best of what you have got!

It is impossible to measure objectively the impact of abundance or scarcity in a child's early life. It is possible to suggest that the invisible continuum of scarcity and abundance could be experienced in both emotional (love) and material (wealth) terms. Reconnect with your own early experiences and reflect on the impact on you.

The expectations that were stated and unstated

The self-fulfilling prophecy is a powerful phenomenon. In 1948, Robert Merton coined the term self-fulfilling prophecy to describe "A false definition of the situation evoking a behaviour which makes the originally false conception come true."[9] There are two types of self-fulfilling prophecies: the expectations of others and those that are self-imposed. For most young children, parents are the most 'significant others' in their lives. Parental expectations, both stated and unstated, carry huge weight. The *Pygmalion Effect*[10] suggests that the way a child is treated will have a direct impact on their behaviour. This is true in both family situations and in the classroom. When another significant person believes you will behave in a particular way, they may consciously or unconsciously make it happen through their actions or inactions.

> My parents had very different expectations for my brother and for me as a girl.
>
> Everything I achieved was only considered normal.
>
> My father had very high expectations of me and yet I knew his love was unconditional.

The educational experience that was chosen

The *Pygmalion Effect* in the family and in the classroom is alluded to above. As an 'educational professional', I have had experience of a wide range of educational provision. One of my most interesting experiences as an Inspector, was to visit parents who were home-educating their children. In my professional view these parents were doing almost everything wrong educationally and yet their children were both thriving and learning. Could this have been the combination of unconditional love and high expectations? A small percentage of my interviewees were educated privately, and this points to the socio-economic status of the family and the financial priorities they had chosen.

> My parents supported me, sent me to private school and were very proud of my achievements.
>
> My teachers were very developmentally orientated, and their positive attitude had a significant effect on me.
>
> My independent school emphasised the fact that we are here to serve others.

In summary, Reflection Point 1 provides you with an invitation to consider your upbringing. The four elements I have chosen to focus upon – love, socio-economic circumstances, expectations, and educational experiences - may have relevance for you or you may wish to consider other elements you believe to be more significant in your childhood.

History Reflection Point 2 – Role Models and Encouragement

Role models come in all sorts of shapes and sizes and appear at various points in our life. It is interesting to look back over your personal history and identify the people who have had the greatest influence upon you. "Being a role model is the most powerful form of educating."[11] The four most significant role models in my life were my mother and father, my boss when I was a deputy head teacher and my PhD supervisor. The common characteristic my role models all shared was their ability and willingness to encourage and motivate.

My family life was characterised by unconditional love. I was an unexpected and much wanted post-war baby. Victor Hugo put it succinctly – "The supreme happiness of life is the conviction that we are loved; loved for ourselves, or rather in spite of ourselves."[12] It never occurred to me that it could be otherwise. With the benefit of hindsight, I can trace the attributes and influence of both my parents. My mother had insatiable energy and an extremely positive mindset. She also had high expectations and aspirations for me. My father was highly educated and a great reader. He had a wide range of practical and intellectual skills and was much more easy-going. I believe my father was an excellent coach, although he would never have used that terminology. They were a constant source of encouragement throughout my childhood and adulthood, continuing till their respective deaths.

Professionally, my boss (Fred Brodie) when I was a deputy head teacher, had a huge impact upon my career. He was quite different to the head teachers I had previously met. His professionalism and love of children were inspirational. He had a profound impact on my future behaviour as a senior leader in education. I aspired to lead and manage in the way that he did – to be caring, reflective and progressive. His primary motivation was to make a difference in the lives of the children and staff in his care. I worked closely with him for three years and his influence has lasted a lifetime.

During the period I was working with Fred, he encouraged me to embark upon a part-time MA at Loughborough University. Serendipitously, I was interviewed by Professor Louis Cohen, and he persuaded me to study his Educational Research Methods Module. This was a transformational experience that facilitated my future academic studies. Lou was an inspirational teacher and a great enthusiast. I discovered that he had come late to his academic career and had an insatiable desire to write. Even on holiday, he set himself a daily writing challenge. He agreed to supervise my MA Dissertation and suggested I went on to undertake a PhD. Once again, he agreed to be my supervisor. His tutorials were the most energising experiences of my professional life. I aspired to be like him!

"Set your goals, know your worth, and hold on to the people who care about you. Those people can be your foundation when your life is shaky. They can be role models when you aren't sure how to act. They can be the family you choose when you miss the family you lost." In her book *No Ordinary Liz*[13], Elizabeth Sutherland describes her incredible journey to survive foster care and discover her identity. The book is part memoir and part guidebook, as Liz unravels her complicated past and highlights the impact of role models in her life.

I have identified my four role models as I seek to unravel my past – who are the significant role models in your life? Here is a selection of apposite quotations from my interviewees.

> My role models are my wife, two of my 'systems thinking' tutors and the Professor of Geriatrics who inspired me.

> My key influences are my mum and my wife who demonstrate tolerance and value the idea of freedom.

> The key influences in my life were an auntie who saw the value of education, my Captain in Boys' Brigade and my pastor.

> My father was awe-inspiring, and I spent my early life trying to crawl out from underneath him.

Encouragement

Encouragement is a word that popped up in many of the interviews. People may have different understandings and definitions of what it has meant for them, nevertheless it appears to be a powerful golden thread. Maya Angelou put it beautifully when she said, "I've learned that people will forget what you said, people will forget what you did, but people will never forget how you made them feel."[14] We all love to be encouraged and we are very fortunate indeed to have had committed encouragers in our lives. I have asked hundreds of people on leadership development programmes to identify the people who have influenced them most. The challenge is usually framed as three questions:

» Who are the three or four people who have had the greatest influence on your life?

» What did they do or say that influenced you?

» How did they make you feel?

I agree with Maya Angelou that feelings are indeed facts. The way people make you feel is enormously powerful. Ask yourself the three questions above and reflect on your answers. The dictionary definition of encourage is "to give courage, confidence, or hope"[15]. Impressionable children and sophisticated adults respond similarly to encouragement, it appears to have a galvanising effect on behaviour. It would seem people crave encouragement.

> I regret that I was not encouraged more as a child. Encouragement is about reminding people that they are good at things.

> My parents were not great encouragers.

> I was greatly influenced by my history teacher, who was a professional who went above and beyond.

> I was never told I was good.

History Reflection Point 3 – Formative Experiences

Most of my interviewees highlighted the significance of early experiences that continued to shape their later lives. I have already identified the impact of parenting, the significance of role models and the power of encouragement. Four other recurring themes emerged that merit further attention, although they may have already been touched upon. They are:

» School experiences

» Health considerations

» The role of competition

» Significant people

Young children in this country are required to leave the confines of their family setting before the age of five and to enter the world of formal education. This may be nursery, playschool, or statutory infant education. This is a significant transition, a different world with different expectations and challenges. School is a completely new experience, with different rules and ways of behaving. I can vividly remember my first day at primary school. The memories are about the people - the other children and the teacher. During those early years, I learned to read, write, and do arithmetic. I also learned to navigate the playground and to look after myself. I did labour under the challenge of having my father as the head teacher!

Children arrive at school from different home settings and have a variety of challenges to deal with. Two of my interviewees highlighted the impact of physical health on educational experience and subsequent view of the world. The necessity of undergoing a series of operations shaped one person's early years and generated a life-long desire to support the underdog.

> I had a whole series of operations as a child and this experience encouraged me to support people in the shadows and ultimately shaped who I was as a teacher.

Another interviewee recounted a life-threatening medical condition that caused her to value life and develop a mindset that emphasises making the most of every day. In Chapter 5, I will return to the significance of 'health wealth' and the fact that we often take good health for granted until it disappears.

I had Hodgkinson's Disease at 18 and it changed the way I think. I decided to make the most of every day.

My primary school was set up on very traditional lines and the 11+ examination was the end point of my formal primary education. This was the norm at that time. The environment was highly competitive, with regular tests and annual examinations. The class seating plan was based on test performance and so you could immediately see where you featured in the peer group pecking order. Competition was deemed to be a significant motivator of high performance. (The role and nature of competition has featured as a very emotive theme in my life as a teacher and trainer of teachers.) I often ask myself, was I born competitive, did my parents encourage me to be competitive, or did these early educational experiences sharpen the desire to compete? Sport played an increasingly large part in my primary school life with the ultimate aspiration of getting into the school football team.

I realised I had a very competitive nature that I did not want to own up to. My degree did not stir me, but my teaching career did, and I realised I am very competitive in a work situation.

For me, secondary school saw another increase in my understanding of the pressure competition exerts. Different subjects, different teachers, and different competitors. It was a single-sex school with a lot of academic and sporting competition. As an August birthday, I was one of the youngest in my year group. Malcolm Gladwell[16] believes birth date is a very significant influence on success. He discovered that a disproportionate number of successful ice hockey players were born toward the beginning of the school year. Maturity provides obvious mental and physical advantages, and the cut-off date of the school year is deeply significant in this context! How do you look back on your secondary education? What memories are etched into your psyche?

I remember two incidents in my first month at secondary school. I was in a music lesson in the assembly hall and my class was clustered around the grand piano at the front of the room. We were each required to sing a short solo. My effort was greeted with a less than favourable response from my music teacher. "You are a groaner, stand at the back and do not sing!" Even with my limited musical education to date, I knew this was not a positive appraisal. This man probably did not realise that my love of music and my willingness to sing in public would be affected by this comment for many years.

The same week I attended the trials for the Under 13 football team and this was the pinnacle of my aspirations. Miraculously I was selected – cue wild celebrations and dancing in the street. The long-lasting consequences of these two episodes is that I have limited enjoyment of music in its various forms and the delusional thought that I can play any sport with a large degree of success. As mentioned earlier, I later discovered this is called the classic self-fulfilling prophecy! **People**, in this case teachers, verbalised their evaluation of my ability and I internalised their appraisals at face value. Their evaluations caused me to see myself in a particular way and these evaluations influenced my later behaviour.

I have asked adult delegates on development programmes about their formative school experiences and highly successful people are often nurturing long-standing scars from the careless words of teachers or classmates. In the interests of balance, it is important to record that lots of my clients and interviewees identify the significance of special teachers on their growth and development. These teachers may have had a profound impact during primary, secondary, or tertiary education.

My values in later life still reflect the influence of my parenting.

A strong work ethic was drummed into me as a child, and I find it hard to understand people who are not committed.

History Reflection Point 4 – The Formation of Your Value System

Our value system underpins a lot of our life choices and ways of being. Our values may come to the surface by default or more often lurk at the unconscious level. They come to light in the behaviours we choose and the priorities we display. Have you ever stopped to interrogate your value system and to examine how it came into being?

Cheryl Richardson presents an exercise in her book *Stand up for your life*[17] designed to help you define your core values. This exercise has been replicated and modified in countless other places and highlights the importance of raising your value system to the conscious level. Values represent the very essence of what is important to us. We are all brought up in family settings or other circumstances that emphasise different values. For example, my respondents identified the significance of a strong work ethic and the power of competition.

My father worked incredibly hard and family life was built around a strong work ethic.

My brother was two years older than me, and we competed with one another from a very early age.

To explore life to the full, you must be prepared to take risks.

My parents manifested a strong Protestant work ethic.

As your author/coach, I suggest that it is helpful to understand the values we were brought up with to decide which of these values are serving us today. Teenagers may rebel against the values of their parents and yet in later life find they are more like their parents than they realised. Alternatively, other influences on our life may lead to the progressive modification of the value system of our younger selves. Either way, it seems a fruitful undertaking to review where we are at this point. We may be able to contrast new ways of seeing the world with the ones we were brought up with. The *World Values Survey*[18] is a global research project that studies values and beliefs. Unsurprisingly, the environment we grow up in, our gender and the socio-economic circumstances of our family influence the values we hold dear. My interview data suggests a range of other factors that influence your value system, such as your faith, your ethnicity, your role models, and the nature of your education.

Understanding how we got to be the person we are today is a complex process and one that feels akin to untangling a ball of knotted string. The themes of life mesh together in a way that at first sight appears unfathomable. My belief is that one end of the ball of string may be our value system and I will explore this contention in Chapter 2. What do you think?

The value system that underpins my thinking and behaviour today bears the hallmarks of a variety of influences that have been shaken and stirred to provide my current way of being. I have mentioned my parents, my early education and the role models who have been influential in my life. Other significant influences have been:

» My secondary and tertiary education
» My professional life

» My wife, children, and grandchildren

» My faith community.

I will allude to my own experiences of these four factors and as you read this section reflect on your own unique history – use my experience as your 'thought starter'.

Secondary and tertiary education

My 'O' and 'A' level examinations were an opportunity to demonstrate mediocre performance levels. Looking back, I wonder whether this was a lack of ability, poor teaching, or a lack of self-confidence. (Teachers usually get the blame for underachievement.) Interestingly in the light of the above self-fulfilling prophecies, my sporting career went from strength to strength. I was Captain of the First XI Soccer Team and played in multiple other sports teams, both inside and outside school. This emboldened me to become a Physical Education teacher.

My training and early years of teaching were a great joy. However, I quickly concluded that 4D outside games on a snowy Monday morning was not my ideal future. Serendipitously my former college tutor suggested that I apply for a job at his children's primary school and my career rapidly moved on from there. I was promoted from Class Teacher to Deputy Head, to Head Teacher, and to Local Authority Inspector in thirteen years.

During this period, I also undertook a BA with the Open University, a part-time MA at Loughborough University, and my PhD (supervised by Lou Cohen, as outlined earlier). These awards provided me with some sense of academic credibility and facilitated the changes in my career. In retrospect, they had a galvanizing impact on my self-confidence. My interest in research was born and is still shining brightly today. It was both a rich period of learning and an elaborate exercise in time management.

My professional life continued to diversify – I led a Management Development Unit for five years and then by chance was invited to be a Head Teacher again. Three headships, part-time lecturer at two universities and a National Leader of Education followed. In 2002 I became a born-again coach and have spent the subsequent years promoting coaching in schools. Through this work my passion for lifestyle development was born! And here we are.

My developing family and spiritual life

I met my wife at college, and we married soon after leaving. We were blessed with three children (they would say 'wonderful children') and moved to a new house five times during their childhood. Most importantly, we became Christians in 1978. We would both identify this as the most significant event in our lives. We have been heavily involved in Christian ministry ever since.

Our Christian belief system underpins our decision making and life choices. For over forty-five years we have attended church every week and listened to over two thousand sermons. The three pillars of our Christian life are daily prayer, bible study and spending time with other members of our faith community. We have undertaken various ministries and served in a wide variety of roles. Most importantly, we have experienced the unconditional love of a God who sent his only son to die for us. "For God so loved the world that he gave his one and only Son, that whoever believes in him shall not perish but have eternal life."[19]

Our belief system is based upon an eternal perspective and the verities of the Christian faith. It would be interesting to analyse the impact our faith has had on the way we have established priorities and invested our time, energy, and money over the past forty plus years.

My wife has been, and is, the inspiration and moral compass in my life. She entertains few shades of grey and has clear views on most things. I believe her to be an excellent mother and grandmother and the communication hub of our wider family network. Our three children have all married and have had children of their own. The three 'non-bloods', an epithet coined by one of our sons-in-law, have brought a new dimension and new ways of thinking to our nuclear family. Our eight grandchildren have been a great blessing and a further extension to our growing family.

In 2020 we established the *Family Learning Community* and this has provided the opportunity to spend time together and to learn together. More on that in Chapter 5.

History Reflection Point 5 – Mindset Development

The mindset that guides our daily decision making and ways of being is influenced by our unique history. As this chapter has rehearsed, we can reflect on our own path through life by choosing to consider its constituent elements. My editorial preference, based on my own life and the interview data I have collected, has settled upon five reflection points:

» The impact of your parenting

» Role models and encouragement

» Formative experiences

» The formation of your value system

» Mindset development

These elements are interactive and refuse to remain static. Mindset development is a dynamic process that reflects among other things, our history, our beliefs, our mood, and our view of the future. Carol Dweck wrote her seminal book entitled *Mindset* in 2006[20] and since that time a range of other authors have built on her original thinking. *Bounce: the myth of talent*[21] is a particularly helpful addition to this genre. Matthew Syed suggests that talent is a bit of a myth and that outstanding performers are good at what they do because they have worked hard at it. I find this view inspiring!

Dweck posits two basic mindsets:

» A **fixed mindset** holds that your qualities are carved in stone. You have a certain level of intelligence, a certain personality, and a certain moral character. This is the hand you have been dealt.

» A **growth mindset** is based on the belief that your basic qualities are things you can cultivate through your own efforts. Everyone can change and grow through experience.

The notion of fixed and growth mindsets has spawned a plethora of educational materials for application in the classroom – it has also shed light on lifestyle development. Positive psychology holds that we can choose to change our mindset regardless of our previous experiences in life. Take a moment to unpackage your own unique mindset - at this moment, on this day.

My core mindset is shaped by my family history. My father and grandfather were miners, and my family was very resilient in adversity. I struggle with people who are not resilient!

We can change our mindset and as leaders we can influence the mindset of others. Focusing on the positive is the starting point.

It is a personal decision – we decide if the glass is half full or half empty.

People respond to positivity – a sunshine and flowers mindset.

As a committed, life-long learner, I nurture the strong belief that we can choose to change. This is a fundamental tenet of my mindset. John Dewey suggested as far back as 1933 that "We do not learn by experience; we learn from experience as we reflect on it and reconstruct it."[22] Thus, we are presented with a choice point. We can see our history in a determinist, fixed mindset way or we can choose to reconceptualise our response to the events in our past in a growth mindset fashion.

My aspiration is to live out a **development mindset** that involves a pattern of thinking and a way of looking at the world that celebrates opportunities for continuous growth and transformation. As a parent, an educator, a coach, and a human being, I believe it behoves me to embrace personal and familial growth opportunities.

The next four chapters of this book are predicated upon a development mindset and the notion that we have personal choice and agency in what we elect to do. This is not some Pollyanna illusion of a stressless future, but a strong commitment to possibility thinking and continuous improvement. It will involve a bit of effort and application, but the results will be worth it.

Take some time to gather your reflections and learning from this chapter. Your history and life so far are significant, but they are the beginning not the end of your story. Invest some time in journaling your reflections and undertake the two exercises set out below.

Managing My Transitions

Your reflections on your timeline probably identify times of change and transition. Figure 3, based on the work of William Bridges, proposes a way of understanding this process. William Bridges in his book *Managing Transitions*[23] identifies three stages in managing transitions:

>> Ending, losing, letting go

>> The neutral zone

>> New beginning

Ending, losing, letting go

We must accept that something is ending before we can move on to a new place. This phase is often characterised by fear, denial, sadness, uncertainty, or a sense of loss.

The neutral zone (transition)

The bridge between the old and the new - attachment to the old while trying to adapt to the new – can be a time of creativity and innovation. Alternatively, it can be a time of anxiety, resistance, and confusion. The challenge is to manage your journey through the neutral zone – you may be able to do this yourself or you may need someone else's help. For instance, a coach or a trusted friend.

The new beginning

Beginnings involve new understandings, new values, and new attitudes. New beginnings are characterised by a release of energy in a new direction, they are an expression of a fresh identity. Transition is the inner psychological process that people go through as they internalise their new situation.

The strength of the model is that it focuses on transition, not change. Change happens to people even if they do not seek it, for example, significant illness or unexpected redundancy. By contrast, transition is an internal process – it is how we structure our thinking as we go through change. We may see ourselves very differently as we move through different stages of life. Change can happen in the blink of an eye, whereas transitions usually take place more slowly.

My experience as a pre-retirement coach provides a range of examples as to how successfully people move through these three stages. A recurring theme is the significance of life purpose and commitment in embedding the new beginning. My father retired at 65 and it took him 5 years to figure out his purpose – this was a long transition and represented one third of his retirement.

I am in a transition zone and don't feel the need to push into discomfort. That time will come when I decide no more of this current phase.

Exercise 2: My personal timeline

Chart your life so far using a personal timeline model. It is a very simple structure.

» Draw a line across a sheet of A4 (or A3 if you are older)
» Settle on a scale that represents your age
» The events/phases above the line are good times
» The events/phases below the line are times of distress
» The distance above or below the line will represent the significance
» Draw the line for birth to now

This is a subjective exercise, nevertheless it does have the power to illuminate your past in a visual form. List what you consider to be the most significant events in your life to date – you might do this on a separate piece of paper first. Significant events or phases impact our feelings, attitudes, self-image and who we are today.

Invest some time reviewing the power and impact of the things you have identified. You can reframe some of these experiences if you so choose!

Figure 2 A timeline of Life

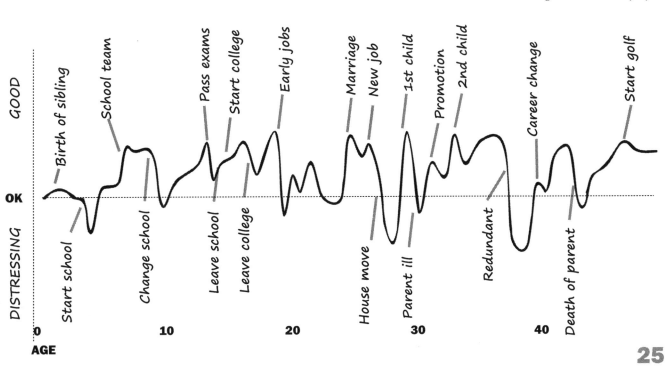

25

Exercise 3: Managing my transitions

Look back at your personal timeline and reflect on the transitions you have made so far. (The first way to attain wisdom according to Confucius.) You have a wealth of experience, some positive, some less so. The challenge is to apply that learning to your future life!

Figure 3 Transitions (after Bridges)

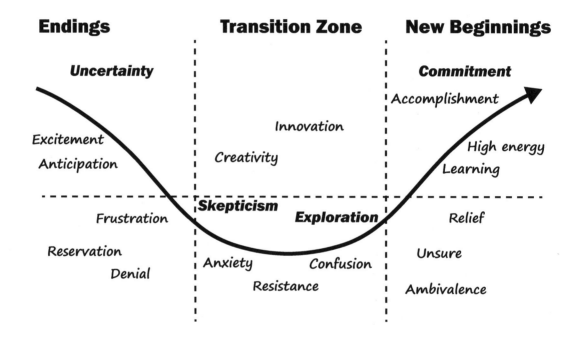

Endings   **Transition Zone**   **New Beginnings**

Uncertainty   *Commitment*

Accomplishment

Innovation

Excitement

Creativity   High energy

Anticipation   Learning

Skepticism   *Exploration*   Relief

Frustration

                                                 Unsure

Reservation   Anxiety   Confusion

Denial   Ambivalence

                          Resistance

Bibliography

1. Laing, R D (1967 The Politics of Experience, 2. St Paul - 1 Corinthians 13:12 (King James Version Bible), 3. Bowlby, J (1953) Childcare and the Growth of Love, 4. Edgar Schein – quotefancy.com, 5. Lipton, B H (2005) The Biology of Belief, 6. Cleese, J (1993) Families and How to Survive Them, 7. George Sand – brainyquote.com, 8. Eleanor Mills – The Daily Telegraph 13.08.21, 9. Merton, R K (1968) Social Theory and Social Structure, 10. Rosenthal, R & Jacobson, L (1968) Pygmalion in the Classroom, 11. John Wooden – goodreads.com, 12. Victor Hugo – brainyquote.com, 13. Sutherland, E (2018) No Ordinary Liz, 14. Maya Angelou – goodreads.com, 15. The Oxford English Reference Dictionary, 16. Gladwell, M (2008) Outliers, 17. Richardson, C (2002) Stand Up for Your Life, 18. World Values Survey 2020 – worldvaluessurvey.org, 19. St John – John 3:16 (New International Version Bible), 20. Dweck, C (2006) Mindset, 21. Syed, M (2011) Bounce: The Myth of Talent, 22.Dewey, J (1933) How We Think, 23. Bridges, W (2017) Managing Transitions: Making the Most of Change.

The future

A time of infinite possibilities

The past has passed. It is banked experience and provides a backdrop to our unique future. What sort of future are you envisioning for yourself? Two of my favourite coaching questions are variations on the same theme.

If a magic wand was waved over you and your ideal future became a reality, what would it be like?

If a miracle takes place while you are asleep and your ideal future has become a reality, what would it be like?

Take a moment to capture the significant elements of your *ideal future* and jot them down in your journal or construct a mind map to summarise them pictorially. This vision of your future gives shape and purpose to your lifestyle choices – unleash your growth mindset energy. "Someday you will rejoice your brave decision to come into the theme park of life refusing to settle for a mediocre ride on the merry-go-round. You chose to go on the big loop roller-coaster instead. So, stop sulking, raise up your hands and enjoy the thrill of the ride!"[1]

In this chapter I would like to invite you to embrace the future you desire and construct the life you would like to lead. The future is of indeterminate length. We know neither the date nor the time that we will quit this mortal coil. We do know that we will not live for ever, so our future does have a boundary, one out of one die! Depending on our age and state of health, it could be imminent or decades away. I imagine I won't think about my grocery shopping or Christmas card lists on my deathbed, but I might think about the state of my relationships with family and friends, and the legacy of my indelible footprint on the world.

Carolyn Hansen, a health and fitness specialist, captures the essence of my aspiration for this chapter. This is how she describes her services on her website: "I help clients take charge of their health before circumstances remove the option. If your quest for peak performance living is a journey, I'll put you in the driver's seat."[2] This chapter is designed is to encourage you to take the driver's seat in planning your future life before it is too late! To live a life by design rather than by default. Stephen Covey rehearses an ancient truism when he asserts that "Most of us spend too much time on what is urgent and not enough time on what is important".[3] Future life planning is about identifying what is important to you.

Examining your past is an interesting prelude to planning your future. Chapter 1, your history, is the springboard for Chapter 2 – your future. "You are reaping today what you have sown in the past and what you sow today will ripen in the future. You are the seed of tomorrow. It is important to know yourself. You must know the minutest details about yourself."[4] Our history influences the way we see the world and our conception of the future possibilities we nurture. Our story so far provides the roots to anchor future growth. Our future tree of life has multiple branches, some already developed boughs and others tender young shoots.

My knowledge of forestry is limited and yet I understand the importance of strong roots below the ground to anchor a flourishing tree above the ground – the part that is visible. The metaphor could be stretched further by highlighting the importance of water, sun, and fertilizer in producing healthy growth. Suffice to say, a thriving tree needs both *roots* and *branches*. A healthy future life draws nourishment from the roots of the past and needs constant shaping and pruning to flourish in the future.

This Chapter is structured around seven key themes. Maintaining the tree analogy, the first three could be seen as strong roots:

» Purpose

» Values

» Mindset

The next four are developing branches of varying length and girth:

» Future learning

» Possibility thinking

» Health wealth

» Peak performance

Purpose

"Dig deep enough in every heart and you'll find a longing for meaning, a quest for purpose. As surely as a child breathes, he will someday wonder, what is the purpose of my life?"[5]

The importance of *purpose* as a strong root of the tree of life was highlighted by one of my interviewees. He was reflecting on his own agnosticism and bemoaned the absence of a faith driver in his life, not least because a strong purpose increases longevity! He was speaking from his perspective as a medic and a researcher. This contention raised my curiosity and caused me to investigate further the impact of purpose.

A cursory review of the literature suggests that people reporting a strong purpose in life, on average, live longer lives than those with a weak purpose. Furthermore, people who lack purpose are 2.4 times more likely to develop Alzheimer's disease than those with a high purpose in life. Physiologically, purpose in life is associated with an increase in natural killer cells that attack viruses and cancerous cells. It would seem sensible to invest time in clarifying your purpose for the health benefits, let alone the wider lifestyle considerations.

Victor Frankl was one of the first to scientifically analyse the existential philosophy of purpose and meaning that can emerge from tragedy. One of the more challenging experiences in my life was a trip to Auschwitz with a Jewish friend. The darkness and atmosphere of the former concentration camp cast a deep shadow over us both. Frankl's description of people and life in such camps was elaborated in his book, *Man's search for meaning*.[7] He describes the amazing powers of endurance of people who have a purpose to go on living and survive the most horrendous circumstances. "He who has a *'why'* to live can bear almost any how." Dr Frankl emphasises man's striving for a higher and ultimate meaning as a reason for continuing to live.

It is noteworthy that within a very different genre, Rick Warren's book *The purpose driven life*[8] has achieved international bestseller status. This Christian book has spawned study groups and sermons dedicated to answering the foundational question: *What am I here for?* Warren believes that "Knowing your purpose gives your life meaning, simplicity, focus and motivation. It also prepares you for eternity."[8] These are bold claims that lead us back to the genetically imprinted quest for purpose within all of us. Although coming from very different starting points, both Frankl and Warren underscore the centrality of purpose.

A less well-known book, but in my view a beautifully written and immensely challenging one, is the work of Victor J Strecher. Surprise, surprise, **purpose** features in the title: *Life on purpose*. The subtitle captures the spirit of the book: *How living for what matters most changes everything*.[9] The author combines science, philosophy, and personal tragedy to illuminate the importance of purpose in life and challenges us (the readers) to find ours. The sudden death of his teenage daughter caused him and the rest of his family to stop taking life for granted and to start living life on purpose. He realised that life is short and so it is important to make the most of it.

One of my interviewees put it very succinctly. She said:

I have decided to say 'Yes' to life and to embrace every opportunity and invitation that comes my way!

Our challenge is to figure out how to make the most of life. Researchers have emphasised the importance of goal–setting since time immemorial and we are all very familiar with the concept in a work context. In earlier books, I have highlighted the difference between *being* and *doing* goals in our personal lives. We are designed to be *human beings* not *human doings*. Goals provide a focus, a destination to be aimed for. Clear goals enhance performance by increasing motivation and effort. Dreams need a plan to turn them into a reality. Clarity of purpose is the preamble to focused goal setting. Life can be very complicated and yet clarity of purpose does not have to be. The exercise at the end of this chapter provides a template for clarifying your values and life purpose. I recommend that you devote time and energy to undertaking this foundational piece of lifestyle planning.

Victor Strecher[9] suggests one way of clarifying the purpose of your life, and the goals that will turn it into a reality, is to undertake the 'headstone test'. When you have died and your headstone has been erected on your grave, what exactly do you want it to say? This is an excellent way of deciding what is important and what is not! Purpose creates the context and parameters of personal goal setting. I take time at the beginning of every academic year to construct a mind-map that summarises my goals for that year. These goals, both *being* and *doing*, reflect the purpose of my life as I have conceptualised it.

Values

Reflection Point 1 in the first chapter raised questions about the formation of our value system. I suggested four elements that had been significant for me and my interviewees:

» Secondary and tertiary education

» Professional life

» Family

» Faith community.

Our value system reflects both our nature and our nurture, and its genesis is very difficult to pin down. In one sense its origins are not as significant as its impact on our behaviour and decision-making both now, and in the future. It is rare for people to externalise and codify their value system, rather it can be inferred from observable behaviour. It is reasonable to conclude that values have a significant role to play in determining who we are, what we want and how we live. "If we dare examine our decisions, we will see our values woven in and through every single one of them. Therefore, it would do us well to take an occasional peek to ensure that our values remain at their peak."[10]

My purpose in highlighting values as a significant component in planning your future is to invite you to raise your current value system to the conscious level. Loch Kelly in his book *Shift into freedom* emphasises the importance of 'open-hearted awareness'. "We all have the capacity to awaken and to live a full life."[11] He likens this process to upgrading your own mental software by awakening your awareness. So, as you verbalise your current value system, what do you notice? For example, one of my interviewees attaches great value to lifelong learning and therefore devotes time to research and educational events.

The knowledge that exists is compulsively interesting...the choice of what to learn becomes more and more important.

Another interviewee identified a strong work ethic modelled by his parents during his childhood. It is not clear whether this was seen as a positive or a negative.

In my value system it is important to drive yourself! I was brought up to serve others unstintingly.

We are brought up in settings that promote certain values, and we cannot simply expunge them from our world view. Nevertheless, by raising these values to the conscious level, we can decide whether we are still committed to these values or want to modify them. I often ask my clients the question 'Is this value serving you or hindering you?'

People experience discomfort and cognitive dissonance when they are asked to behave in ways that conflict with their value system. This is unsurprising as "Your value system is the core of who you are."[12] It is much easier to make decisions once you are clear about the value system that underpins the process for you. Purpose and values are inextricably linked. As Frankl discovered[7] people who have a why survived when seemingly physically stronger people did not. Simon Sinek also emphasises the power of why from a different perspective in his TED talk based on his popular book *Start with why*.[13] Sinek is an unshakable optimist who believes in a bright future and our ability to build it together. Clarifying your WHY (your purpose) inspires you to act and build the future you desire, both personally and collectively.

"It is very important for people to know themselves and understand what their value system is, because if you don't know what your value system is, then you don't know what risks are worth taking and which ones are worth avoiding."[14] When you start a journey, navigation becomes easier when you know the destination. Traversing new territory requires a map and a compass. The destination and the journey could be conceptualised as your purpose. The map and the compass could be seen as your values. "It is not hard to make decisions once you know what your values are."[15]

I have been enthralled by both series of the BBC Two programme *Race Across the World*.[16] Five pairs of contestants are required to navigate thousands of miles to a defined destination. The competitors are not allowed to fly but are each given a money belt containing the amount of money equivalent to a flight to that destination. They are provided with a map, and they can supplement their finances by working during the journey. They have choice about the route and the method of travel. They compete to reach checkpoints along the way and to win the ultimate prize of £20 000. Interesting choices are made about how much sight-seeing and leisure to build into their route. This sounds like life! Get to the destination first or concentrate on enjoying the journey? One of the most dispiriting quotes I have ever read is attributed to Ron Goldman, the founder of Kodak, in his very concise suicide note: "My work is done, why wait?"[17]

I believe Goldman was suffering extreme pain and decided this was his best course of action. In the normal circumstances of life "A highly developed value system is like a compass. It serves as a guide to point you in the right direction when you are lost."[19] In your race across the world or your ascent of the tree of life, it is worth clarifying the values driving you. As identified in Chapter 1, *The*

World Values Survey[19] is a global research project that regularly studies peoples' values and beliefs. As you might expect, wealthier people throughout the world are more likely to value wealth and success than those less well–off financially. However, one of the most important values across all countries and incomes is helping others. The Survey suggests that the country you grow up in and whether you have a large or small bank account influence the values you hold dear and ultimately the purpose in life you create. In short, "Your value system is a revelation of the destination that inspires your journey."[20]

Mindset

Our mindset reflects the values we hold dear. One description of mindset is the belief system we adopt to process information. We carry this software programme in our brain to monitor and interpret incoming information. We respond either consciously or unconsciously to what is happening to us, based on our prevailing programme. In decision and general systems theory, a mindset is a set of assumptions, methods or notions arising from a person's world view.

In the last chapter, I identified five elements to consider in seeking to understand our own mindset and you may wish to flick back to these:

- » The impact of our parenting
- » Role models and encouragement
- » Formative experiences
- » The formation of our value system
- » Mindset development

As frequently restated, this book is predicated upon a growth mindset and the notion that we have personal choice and agency in what we elect to do. I am totally committed to future learning and possibility thinking. We can choose to change our prevailing mindset. This is likely to be an incremental rather than an instantaneous transformation. Changing your mindset is like climbing stairs - it is safer to climb one step at a time, or two if you are feeling excessively energetic! "Vision is not enough. It must be combined with venture. It is not enough to stare up the steps, we must also step up the stairs."[21]

Take time to observe your own behaviour and deduce the underpinning mindset it reveals. This is an investment that will pay rich dividends. The challenging question is how do we change our prevailing mindset? There is a growing body of opinion that practices like mindfulness and meditation will release us from the shackles of a negative or pessimistic mindset. The popularity of the *Headspace* App[22] bears testimony to the exponential growth of these practices. "Mindfulness gives freedom from negative and fixed mindsets to positive and growth mindsets."

My personal meditation journey was galvanised by studying Emily Fletcher's Audible Programme – *Stress less, accomplish more.*[24] She believes meditation is like taking your brain to the gym. The *Ziva Technique* she espouses has three component parts designed to reduce stress in your past, present and future life:

- » Mindfulness
- » Meditation
- » Manifesting.

Mind management is a challenge for most of us and this three-part technique has a delicious simplicity to it.

Mindfulness brings your mind into the present moment and locates you in the NOW. I use the 'coming to your senses' exercise to listen, see, feel, taste and smell what is going on at this moment. In essence this practice is designed to awaken the left part of the brain and provide a doorway into the present.

Meditation facilitates surrender to the NOW and liberates you from the stress of the past. Neuroscience is catching up with what meditators have known for thousands of years about how the mind influences stress. Fletcher suggests that mental hygiene (meditation) should become habitual, like oral hygiene – brush at least twice daily.

Manifesting is designed to get you clear on your future dreams. What is my purpose, what values drive me, and what mindset should I nurture? Starting from a place of gratitude changes the chemistry of your brain. As the saying goes, 'neurons that fire together, wire together'.

I claim no deep knowledge of these techniques, but I have a sense of their usefulness. You may already be an accomplished meditator or successful manifester, I simply challenge you to review your mindset development and your future mind management strategies.

One mind state that has fascinated me for years is the concept of 'flow'. I read Mihaly Csikszentmihalyi's seminal book[25] over 20 years ago and was captivated by the notion that the most satisfying experiences in life are when we are in flow. In flow, purpose and goals are clear. The relationship between goal and action is perfect and the resulting focus and satisfaction is self-rewarding – autotelic. *Autotelic* is derived from the Greek words *auto* (self) and *telos* (goal or purpose).

Csikszentmihalyi's work has spawned numerous other offerings in the pantheon of the self-development literature. One such book is Clyde Brolin's book *In the zone*.[26] He seeks to deconstruct how champions think – the mindset they develop. The three-part approach is a useful starting point – conceive, believe, achieve. This is a framework we can all use:

» The future I desire

» The mindset to facilitate it

» The manifestation of the dream.

The 2006 film *The Holiday*[27] is a romantic comedy that captures an essential truth about mindset development. In the movie, the elderly screen writer Arthur Abbott (Eli Wallach) suggests to the hapless Iris Simpkins (Kate Winslet) that she needs to become 'the leading lady in your own life'. This chimes with insights from my interviewees – *I am the expert in my own life*. I am unique and no one else knows what is going on inside my head. My roots are under the surface, but it is my decision as to which branches to prune or grow!

Let us examine the nature of your branches in a bit more detail. I have chosen to focus on four significant ones:

» Future learning

» Possibility thinking

» Health wealth

» Peak performance

Future learning

Many of my interviewees, regardless of their age or stage, espoused a powerful desire to keep learning. The Khan Academy[28] has tapped into this desire for continuous learning and proudly trumpets "Whoever you are, wherever you are, you only have to know one thing: you can learn anything." This is a bold assertion, but I applaud the underlying philosophy. As both a teacher and a learner during my entire adult life, I have experienced learning challenges both first-hand and second-hand. More importantly, I have experienced the sheer joy of learning.

My primary, secondary and tertiary formal education has been elaborated at some length in Chapter 1 and I invited you to reflect upon your own education. The informal part of the learning journey also merits close attention as it often accrues unnoticed. For example, how do we learn about social relationships and our ability to interact with others? Self-awareness and awareness of others are the twin pillars of successful human relationships, and we have a myriad of opportunities to observe and reflect upon these elements of learning every day. Indeed, self-awareness and awareness of others are often cited as critical factors in the development of successful leaders and are therefore probed in some depth at selection interviews. The future offers the opportunity to do things differently and the learning opportunities are infinite.

> *The choice of what to learn becomes more and more important as we grow older.*
>
> *My approach to life is to build on my strengths and manage my weaknesses.*
>
> *My core purpose in life is helping people develop and grow. This involves enabling them to unlock the potential inside them.*
>
> *I want to learn Spanish, the piano and take a degree with The Open University.*

What would you like to learn next? I am currently engaged in learning to juggle and to draw (not at the same time). These undertakings were inspired by Tom Vanderbilt's book *Beginners*.[29] His writing illustrates the joy and transformative power of lifelong learning as he grapples with the new challenges of playing chess, surfing, singing in a choir, drawing, painting, and wild swimming. The book is a celebration of deliberately moving outside your comfort zone to embrace new learning. The narrative describes in some detail the highs and lows of his learning journeys and cleverly unpicks how the brain learns. "The last, and most important, lesson was that it was never too late to be a beginner."[29]

Our education system reveres examination success as proof that learning has taken place. In this country learners have more measuring points (tests) than virtually any other nation in the world. Children are measured upon entry to formal education and are analysed at various stages until they emerge from the far end of the educational sausage machine. As a former sausage maker, I am acutely aware of the importance to the individual and to the institution of the examination results achieved. Learning provides a key to future success. Externally validated progress (examination results) forms a significant part of our curriculum vitae and, more importantly, could influence our self-image. It did in my case. Learning how to learn and having the self-confidence to move outside your comfort zone are foundational to future success and enjoyment. Regardless of your learning history, you can choose how and what you want to learn in the future.

My foray into drawing has been supported by the work of Betty Edwards.[30] Her book, *Drawing on the right side of the brain*, cleverly combines a drawing primer and a gentle exploration of elements of neuroscience. My drawing experiences have been both a joy and a revelation and I have concluded that learning works best when it is like that. Artistic confidence is the out-working of inner self-talk. One of Tom Vanderbilt's drawing teachers captured this principle perfectly. "A lot of the skills I am teaching are about the way you talk to yourself, about inserting more positive voices in your head rather than the ghosts we all have."[29]

Get rid of the critical ghosts and turn up the volume on the positive voices. I first embraced the world of juggling over two decades ago when a random Christmas present appeared – a pack of three juggling balls. I gritted my teeth and embarked upon a vigorous training session inspired by a flimsy one-page sheet included in the pack. The instruction sheet was entitled simply *How to juggle*. My wife watched my strivings with increasing amusement until she could bear it no longer and relieved me of the frequently dropped torture balls. "This how it is done!" Marital disharmony ensued but she did encourage me to see successful juggling in my mind's eye. This advice was the key!

My reflections on this episode and my subsequent actions are an interesting window into my approach to learning. The competitor in me was committed to achieving a basic level of success, after all I can shine at almost anything involving a ball! More seriously, my default learning strategy was to research the subject and the purchase of *Lessons from the art of juggling*[31] quickly ensued. The insights in this tome accelerated my juggling prowess and caused me to review the whole business of adult learning.

The inside cover of the book proclaims that the insights it contains will train the reader in the art of relaxed concentration – the secret of high performance in business and life. *Lessons from the art of juggling* was published in 1995 and provided an approach to self-development based on the latest brain and learning research. Learning to deliberately drop the ball breaks down mental/brain barriers to making mistakes and opens new pathways to perception. I had had plenty of practice at dropping the balls and my immediate conclusion was that this was a great way of engaging delegates on my leadership development programmes. It was!

Is the juggling episode an exemplar of my approach to future learning?

» Have a go (active learning)

» Do some research, read a book, attend a course (expert teaching)

» Apply the insights (pragmatic learning)

» Deliberate practice (embedded learning)

Learning to learn is a journey that never ends as nothings stays still. The development of neuroscience is changing the learning landscape, technology moves on apace and our own approaches to learning are constantly evolving as we grow and develop. To grow even stronger, our 'learning muscles' need exercise. How much attention are you lavishing upon yours? 'The art of learning'[32] charts the inner journey to optimal performance of the author Josh Waitzkin. The in-depth analysis of his road to international success in both chess and the martial arts is an inspiring read. "In life, I worked on embracing change instead of fighting it. With awareness and action, in both life and chess my weakness was transformed into strength."[32]

Waitzkin personifies someone committed to being the best he could be in his chosen areas of endeavour. He identified awareness and action as fundamental to his success. I have highlighted the importance of awareness and responsibility in my earlier books, and I believe the differences are more semantic than philosophical. Review your own progress in learning to learn and taking responsibility for implementing the action that is generated by this review. I have long believed that if learners could avoid making the same mistakes, both technical and psychological, their progress would skyrocket. Relaxed concentration is key in successful learning – juggle without worrying about what your hands are doing! How do you get yourself into 'the zone' where optimal learning takes place?

Waitzkin's view is in tune with the quotation of my second interviewee earlier. "In my experience the greatest of artists and competitors are masters of navigating their own psychologies, playing on their strengths, controlling the tone of battle so that it fits with their personalities."[32] Maximise your strengths and minimise your weaknesses. This is the essence of living a conscious lifestyle!

Possibility thinking

> "A man will be imprisoned in a room with a door that's unlocked and opens inwards; as long as it does not occur to him to pull rather than push it." Ludwig Wittgenstein[33]

Possibility thinking starts from the premise that there are no locked doors, although at first sight it may appear so! The notion of unlocking potential is a powerful one that is often espoused during selection interviews. What untapped possibilities do you feel reside within you – which acorn could grow into your proverbial oak tree?

Possibility thinking could be perceived as a dimension of your prevailing mindset. At the simplest level, it could be defined as the willingness to see possibilities rather than limitations. One of my coaching clients is undertaking a research study to uncover the benefits that have accrued to secondary schools from the Covid 19 pandemic. This is a great example of seeing the possibilities embedded within a challenging problem and a willingness to search out and learn from the positive elements.

When a new idea is presented or a new experience is offered, the default position is to identify the possibilities rather than the problems or blockages. One way of assessing the culture of a team or the level of an individual's possibility quotient is to observe responses to a proposal to do things differently. At the simplest level, there are often two classically different responses – *yes but* or *yes and*. *Yes but* people home in on all the reasons why the proposal will not work: *We've tried it before*, *Not with our people*, *It will cost too much* and so the blocking goes on. The *yes and* group start from a different place and look for all the opportunities – *That could work*, 'That's a great idea and what we could also do is, *Let me add to that great suggestion*. The *yes but* people are a demolition gang, while the *Yes and* group are a construction team. What is your default position?

We usually have far more choices than we realise – the challenge is to open our eyes wide enough to see them. Our *Reticular Activating System* (RAS) is designed for this precise purpose. When I commit to finding the opportunities in every situation, my RAS is engaged and open for business. The RAS is an automatic goal seeking mechanism located in the brain and it is designed to search for possibilities, but it needs to be programmed properly. To quote H Jackson Brown Jr., "Opportunity dances with those who are already on the dance floor."[34] He is emphasising that we need to be in the right state to make the most of the opportunities that present themselves. Firstly, we need to be able to recognise the potential dance partner and secondly, we need the courage to ask for the dance. The reticular activating system needs to be fully open to spot potential partners and see the possibilities inherent in the dance.

I would love to change the world. So much to do and so little time!

To explore life to the full, you need to take risks and embrace the possibilities life throws up.

The best is yet to come!

My mindset is to be an optimistic doer.

These four interviewees have certainly embraced the notion of possibility thinking and the fourth quotation emphasises the importance of optimism. We have a fundamental choice in the way we approach the future. We can see boundless possibilities beckoning us on or we can focus on pessimistic predictions about the things to be endured.

Nelson Mandela is an inspiring example of someone who chose to focus on the positive.

> **"I am fundamentally an optimist. Whether that comes from nature or nurture, I cannot say. Part of being optimistic is keeping one's head pointing towards the sun, one's feet moving forward. There were many dark moments when my faith in humanity was sorely tested, But I would not and could not give myself up to despair. That way lays defeat and death."[3]**

Nelson Mandela personifies possibility thinking – from a prison cell on Robben Island to the South African Presidential Residence. Despite his incarceration, Mandela managed to retain his relentless optimism about future possibilities. In his book *Learned optimism*, Martin Seligman[3] suggests than we can learn to be optimistic despite the external circumstances. His theory of success suggests people need three characteristics:

» Aptitude – the talent

» Motivation - the desire

» Optimism - the magic ingredient.

Are the characteristics of possibility thinking similar?

» Aptitude – the ability to identify possibilities.

» Motivation – the desire to make the most of every situation.

» Optimism – the ability to focus on the positive.

Possibility thinking is a golden thread that runs through the intention to live a conscious lifestyle and it will keep popping up in later sections of this book!

Health Wealth

Possibility thinking is fundamental in the recovery from ill health, both mental and physical. People often take good health for granted and only accord it serious thought when it is disappears. Think about how good a healthy leg feels after an extended time on crutches – sickness is the most potent ambassador for healthy living. Health and wellbeing are topics that are attaining an ever-higher profile in both the home and workplace. Never more so than during a worldwide pandemic!

Financial wealth is measurable in terms of the amount of money and things you possess and can be described numerically. Health wealth is a much more slippery concept that is harder to measure accurately. Healthy lifestyle proponents suggest that a focus on your own mental and physical wellbeing is the key to longevity, success, and quality of life. No small claims.

Ironically my first significant wake-up call arrived after a trip to *The O2* to enjoy the *ATP Tennis Finals*. My back began to ache as I watched world class athletes doing their thing. Over three days, it continued to become more painful till my movement was restricted, my sleep wrecked, and I reluctantly concluded that I needed to act. My first ever visit to an osteopath ensued, followed by a visit to the GP and eventually an MRI scan. I also implemented my go to learning strategy and bought two books on back pain. Lack of sleep and an increasing level of pain underscored the significance of the mind-body connection.

I am not sure whether I read about the concept of **health wealth** or if it was an obvious response to my current predicament. I swallowed increasing amounts of pain killers, paid more visits to the osteopath, and religiously performed the exercises prescribed. The breakthrough arrived in the form of a saviour physio-therapist at Bisham Abbey National Sports Centre. She had previously worked wonders on my wife's back troubles and was able to do the same for mine.

This three-month back pain episode caused me to stop and think, to research preventative medicine and to modify my lifestyle. I concluded that as in other areas of life, knowledge is potential power. We can equip ourselves with both the knowledge and the resources needed to take ownership of our mental and physical health. We cannot control accidents or chronic illness, but we can make a difference to our current state of health. I also reluctantly accepted that my body was getting older, weaker, and needed more care and attention!

My desire for health wealth has unconsciously led me to a three-year research programme delving further into the components of a healthy mind and body. Dr Victor Strecher mentioned earlier in this Chapter[6] proposes that the mnemonic SPACE is a handy way of remembering five components of robust health – *Sleep, Presence, Activity, Creativity, Eating.*

Sleep

The significance of sleep only became fully apparent to me by its absence. I had taken sleep for granted. How much sleep do you need? The gift of an Apple Watch enabled me to track my sleep and to know when to feel tired! Sleep, or more accurately lack of it, is a big issue for lots of people – the failure to get to sleep or the inability to get back to sleep after waking prematurely. The sub-title of Ariana Huffington's book *The Sleep Revolution*[37] underscores the challenge: *Transforming your life, one night at a time.* Lack of sleep has profound consequences for our health, happiness, performance, and relationships. Brain health is directly impacted by a lack of revitalising sleep – the healthy brain needs time to repair and reboot. Most of us need between 7 and 8 hours of sleep in a 24-hour period.

Does your sleep need attention?

Presence

Earlier in this chapter, the *three Ms* were outlined in some detail – *Mindfulness, Meditation* and *Manifesting.* Presence involves a combination of all three and can be defined as paying attention to the current moment in a sustained way. The popular *Headspace App*[35] highlights the power of being non-judgementally present in the moment and encourages the ability to observe your own thinking and feeling. Back to what my old friend Csikszentmihalyi[25] would describes as *in flow*, or as Brolin[25] conceptualises the state, *in the zone.* The coaching literature emphasises the importance of being *fully present* and as a coach I endeavour to achieve that state – body and mind in the same place. It is equally as important in everyday life! Are you able to sustain presence? (The final chapter of this book addresses the power of NOW in much more detail.)

Activity

This book is predicated upon the desire to live an active and fulfilling lifestyle. What does that look like for you? Later in this chapter I will invite you to undertake the *Wheel of Life exercise.* This task is designed to support you in clarifying your thinking about what you choose to be the active components of your life. For example, the spokes of the wheel may be designated as your physical, mental, and spiritual health, and so on. Where do you want to increase or decrease your attention and allocation of energy?

Creativity

I have long believed that the arts are a vital part of a rounded education, for both children and adults. My engagement in speaking, writing, and drawing are the outworking of a desire to express my own brand of creativity. I have already mentioned the impact of Betty Edwards[30] and I would also like to highlight the work of Julia Cameron[38]. I have studied her books and engaged in her on-line programme. The New York Times said of Cameron that she 'invented the way for people to renovate the creative soul'. A high accolade indeed and it worked for me. *How do you renovate your creative soul?*

Eating

Eating is one of life's great pleasures, especially when accompanied by fine wine and engaging company. Quite by chance three years ago, I took my wife on a random bargain-break to Grayshott Manor. I had not realised it was a Health and Wellness Spa until I attempted to order a beer! A lunch-time lecture by Stephanie J Moore proved compelling. Her title: *Why eating less and exercising more makes you fat.*[39] This lunchtime lecture inspired us to attend the week-long programme the following summer – a truly transformational and conscious lifestyle experience. The key message: everyone that eats has a 'diet' – what is the nature of yours?

Back to the subject of **health wealth** and the imperative to evaluate your current state of health and wellbeing. I suggest you reflect on three aspects of subjective wellbeing – evaluative, hedonic, and eudemonic.

> » Evaluative wellbeing (life satisfaction measures)
>
> » Hedonic wellbeing (feelings of happiness, sadness, anger, stress, and pain)
>
> » Eudemonic wellbeing (sense of purpose and meaning in life)

Both subjective wellbeing and health are closely linked to age. The *Gallup Global Wellbeing Survey*[40], a continuing survey in more than 150 countries, shows a U-shaped relation between evaluative wellbeing and age in high-income, English-speaking countries, with the lowest levels of wellbeing in ages 45-54 years. The relationship between physical health and wellbeing is bidirectional. Older people with chronic illnesses unsurprisingly show increased levels of depressed mood and impaired hedonic and eudemonic wellbeing. Most interestingly the Survey suggests a possible association between wellbeing and a protective role in health maintenance. In my lay-person terms, this underscores the relevance of **health wealth** and the importance of prioritising the optimisation of our health and wellbeing.

It could be argued that the safety net of our beloved NHS encourages us to be lazy about our own health and wellbeing – if something goes wrong the medical professionals will 'fix' it. My reason for highlighting the role of **health wealth** in living a conscious lifestyle, is to encourage us all to be proactive in our daily choices. As we age it becomes ever more important to do the things that we know will help us sustain good health and subjective wellbeing for as long as possible.

Casual ageism engenders a prejudice about my older self being inferior to my younger self. This is another potential example of the afore-mentioned self-fulfilling prophecy. All ageing is successful, otherwise you are dead! Ageism is the last socially sanctioned prejudice, and we have a choice about how to respond to manifestations of it. After all, it does not make sense to discriminate against a group we all aspire to join. I prefer to think in terms of living longer rather than growing older. The ageing process is a natural and inevitable one, regardless of expensive creams or the latest exercise programmes – we are all old people in training, despite the protestations of 'baby-boomers'.

I have included this section to emphasise the positive benefits of ageing. Age is a staircase that has the potential to lift us to an understanding of wisdom (one of my core values), relationship, and personal authenticity (another of my core values). As we age our capacity for integration increases and our brains are more diversely wired and possess many more connections. Perhaps recalling names is harder because we have so many more in our memory banks! Good health, good friends and secure finances predispose us to a satisfying and ful-filling lifestyle. **Health wealth** is not just the absence of illness, it is about being the best we can be!

Peak performance

The roots (purpose, values, and mindset) and branches (future learning, possi-bility thinking, and health wealth) of your tree form the future that will facili-tate peak performance. Your life so far has provided you with the data to know how to be the best you can be, whether you realise it or not. Peak performance is about operating at the highest level of your physical and mental capacities – the stimulating quest of a conscious lifestyle.

Anders Ericsson[41] spent his career finding out how peak performers acquire their world-class skills. He studied Olympic athletes, chess grandmasters, re-nowned concert pianists, prima ballerinas, PGA golf champions, radiologists and the lists go on. His notions of *the ten-thousand-hour rule* and *the ten-year rule* have spurned a myriad of research studies as they emphasise the importance of **deliberate practice**. Peak performers do not simply log hours of practice, they practise in a different way – they aim for perfect practice. You have spent a lifetime honing your skills and now is the time to translate that practice into deliberate action!

Back to your roots:

» What is your **purpose** in doing what you are doing?

» What **values** drive your desire to perform at your best?

» What is the **mindset** that underpins your performance?

Your roots provide a firm foundation that will anchor you in the storms and challenges of life. Ten thousand hours of deliberate practice build neural path-ways that will serve you well in the future. Set yourself goals that will stretch you and make them 'just manageable', although they may at first appear out of reach. This level of stress is motivating – facilitative rather than destructive. Excellence is about daring to step outside your comfort zone and embracing the trials and tribulations inherent in growth.

The branches of your future tree are mutually supportive:

» **Future learning** will short-circuit the development of peak performance - learning to learn, how to perform at your best.

» **Possibility thinking** opens new areas of endeavour and levels of performance.

» **Health wealth** provides the energy and resilience to address these new challenges.

Hungarian educational psychologist Laszlo Polgar[41] had always been opposed to the theory of natural talent as the reason for outstanding performance. In the end, he decided the only way to prove that peak performance could be delib-erately nurtured was to prove it with his own children. Despite not yet having children, he boldly asserted that his future offspring would become geniuses. He chose chess as a medium to prove this assertion — echoes of Vanderbilt[29] and Waitzkin[32] mentioned earlier.

Polgar got married and had three daughters: Susan, Sophia, and Judit. At age 4, Susan won her first chess tournament and at 15 became the top-rated female chess player in the world. Sophia is best known for the *Miracle in Rome*, where she won eight games in a row against many of the greatest players of the era. The odds were incredible, and it is still seen as one of the most extraordinary chess performances in history. Judit is considered the best female player of all time. At 14, she became a Grandmaster – the youngest person to have ever done so. She defeated 11 current or former world champions and occupied the number one position for 26 years until she retired in 2015.

Richard Williams, the father of Venus and Serena, nurtured an equally challenging ambition for the success of his daughters. He believed they could be world tennis champions and set a plan in motion to make that belief a reality. And a reality it did become – Venus became a 7-time Grand Slam winner and Serena has so far carried off 23 Grand Slam titles. As a doubles team, the sisters have also had remarkable success, they have won innumerable titles and completed the Career Doubles Golden Slam.

The story of the Williams family has recently been made into a film starring Will Smith. It is entitled *King Richard*[42] and catalogues the early days of the future tennis champions. The editor of the film revealed, "Before taking the job, I knew very little about Richard Williams, and it was mostly filtered through the media — *That crazy dad* or *He's a nut job*. Now I think the guy is a genius." Will Smith was similarly gushing about Richard Williams: "This is a film about family, about faith. It's a film about big dreams, you'd have to be a Grinch to walk out of this film and not be inspired."

The Polgar sisters and the Williams sisters are examples of people achieving international success and world fame. The starting point was the ambition of their parents. John Richardson describes a completely different challenge in his quest for peak performance. His book is aptly entitled *Dream On*[44]. That is exactly what professional golfer Sam Torrance exclaimed when he heard what Richardson was undertaking. Despite Torrance's scepticism, Richardson set himself the challenge of playing a level par round of golf in a year.

The back story is that Richardson had never broken a hundred and had to reduce his best score by 33 shots to achieve his goal. He had a full-time job plus a partner and a young child. With no natural talent, precious little time, and no fitness level to speak of, could it be done? The book charts the ups and downs of his journey, the relentless practice, and the contribution of different coaches. Of course, he achieved his seemingly unattainable goal. On the penultimate page of his book, Richardson concludes that the whole episode was *A challenge to get really good at something in a set period against all the odds. A challenge to fulfil an old childhood dream. A challenge to change my life.*

Three different stories – three stunningly successful outcomes. What is the learning?

The parents, the children and the golfer shared a **passion** for their respective games. Is this the prerequisite of peak performance that you are passionate about what you are doing?

The performers undertook a coherent and sustained training routine of **deliberate practice** to build the skills required to achieve the desired goal. These sessions were overseen by committed and talented coaches.

The four daughters and 'the hacker' all displayed remarkable persistence and commitment in their desire to achieve **peak performance**.

In summary: **passion + deliberate practice = peak performance**

Another element of peak performance is to understand how to get the best out of yourself. Relentless practice is fundamental, but so is the ability to rest. 'What makes the best is the ability to rest' is a prevalent mantra in the field of sports science. Overtraining causes breakdown and exhaustion and the notion of a 'sabbath day rest' is an important one for all of us. Your coach has a role to play in helping you find the right balance. Review your own routines and approaches and evaluate what helps you perform well and what hinders you.

Charles Duhigg explores the importance of routines that serve you in his book *The power of habit*[45]. The key is to understand how habits work in everyday life and armed with this knowledge, to review your own. How about asking yourself some simple questions? Are you a lark or an owl? Do you achieve your best results in the morning or in the evening? Where do you do your best work? Can you manage your moods to put yourself in a resourceful psychological space?

As an example, I have developed my own routine that helps me perform at my best as a public speaker. I endeavour to:

» Research the topic thoroughly – solid preparation.

» Crystallise my thinking over a few days (and nights) – the key learning points.

» Do the inner preparation – practise positive self-talk.

» Deliver confidently – peak performance.

Take some time to analyse how you get yourself into a place to achieve peak performance in any area of your life. Think of recent examples and outline and analyse them in your journal. You have spent days, months and years developing your existing habits, probably mostly at the unconscious level. Now is the time for a sustained review.

Exercise 4: My core values and purpose

It was suggested earlier in the chapter that it is worth 'peeking' at the value system that underpins your life – the life purpose that informs your decision-making and actions.

* Step 1: Read through the word list below and circle the words that are significant to you. If you feel any are missing, add them to the list.

* Step 2: Narrow your list down to your ten most important words.

* Step 3: Reduce the list further to the five most important. Are these your core values?

* Step 4: Take the obituary test – what would you want people to say about you at your memorial service? These reflections are the components of your life purpose.

* Step 5: What are the future goals that matter to you most? Break these down into the key areas of your life. (Use these as the raw materials for the next exercise: The Wheel of Life.)

* Step 6: You have completed the exercise. The challenge is to make the core values and life purpose you have uncovered central to what you do in the future. Summarise the outcomes of this exercise on one sheet of A4 paper and display it in your workspace, write it in your diary and have it on your phone – let it guide future action.

Table 1
Word list for Exercise 4

Abundance	Calmness	Cooperation	Friendship
Acceptance	Capability	Courage	Flexibility
Accomplishment	Challenge	Creativity	Freedom
Accountability	Charity	Credibility	Fun
Achievement	Cheerfulness	Curiosity	Generosity
Adventure	Cleverness	Decisiveness	Glamour
Ambition	Coaching	Dedication	Gratitude
Appreciation	Collaboration	Dependability	Growth
Arousal	Commitment	Diversity	Happiness
Authenticity	Communication	Empathy	Health
Autonomy	Community	Encouragement	Holiness
Balance	Compassion	Enthusiasm	Honesty
Beauty	Competition	Excellence	Honour
Bliss	Congruence	Expertise	Humour
Boldness	Contribution	Family	Imagination
Independence	Loyalty	Professionalism	Spirituality
Innovation	Manifesting	Quality	Stability
Inspiration	Meditation	Recognition	Success
Intelligence	Mindfulness	Religion	Teamwork
Integrity	Motivation	Resilience	Trust
Intuition	Openness	Respect	Understanding
Kindness	Optimism	Responsibility	Usefulness
Knowledge	Passion	Safety	Versatility
Laughter	Personal development	Security	Warmth
Leadership	Playfulness	Selflessness	Wealth
Learning	Popularity	Service	Wellbeing
Love	Power	Simplicity	Wisdom

Exercise 5 My Wheel of Life

This is one of my favourite exercises that has been undertaken by innumerable clients with great success.

Step 1 Look at the example provided below and identify the six to eight spokes that are important in your life.

Step 2 Use Figure 2 to evaluate the length of each of your spokes. Allocate a score to each spoke — 0 is the lowest and 5 is the highest.

Step 3 Draw a line between each spoke to make visible the shape of your 'current reality'. Which spokes are shorter and which ones are longer? How do you feel about the shape of your current life that emerges?

Step 4 A balanced life does not mean making each spoke the same length. You decide what length you want each spoke to be, reflecting both your core values and life purpose. Highlight the spokes where you plan to make changes. This is your action plan for the immediate future.

Step 5 Revisit your Wheel of Life annually and review the changes you have made and ask 'where next?

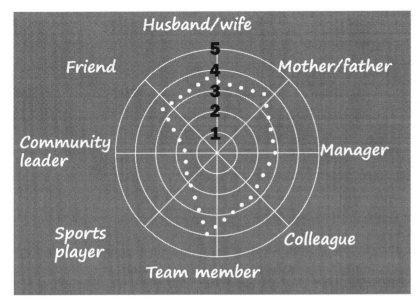

Figure 4 Example Wheel of Life

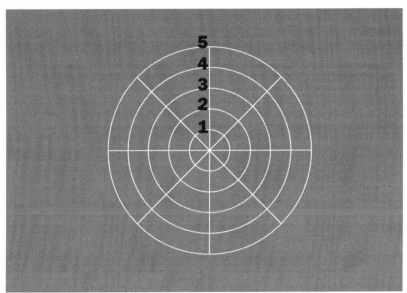

Figure 5 The Wheel of Life to complete

Bibliography

1. St Maarten, A (2012) Divine Living, 2. Carolyn Hansen – carolynhansenfitness.com, 3. Covey, S R (1992) The Seven Habits of Highly Effective People, 4. Awdhesh Singh – goodreads.com, 5. Max Lucado – wow4u.com, 6. Strecher, V J (2016) Life on Purpose, 7. Frankl, V (2004) Man's Search for Meaning, 8. Warren, R (2002) The Purpose Driven Life, 9. Victor Strecher – kumanu.com, 10. Craig Lounsbrough – goodreads.com, 11. Kelly, L (2015) Shift into Freedom, 12. Ofentse Olunloyo – ofentseolunloyo.com, 13. Sinek, S (2009) Start with Why, 14. Benjamin Carson – azquotes.com, 15. Roy Disney - wordpress.com, 16. BBC Two – Series One 2029 & Series Two 2020, 17. Ron Goldman – openculture.com, 18. Idowu Koyenikan – linkedin.com, 19. World Values Survey (2020) – worldvaluesseurvey.org, 20. Albert Avuokeye – leadershipquote.org, 21. Vaclav Havel – leadershipquote.org, 22. Andy Puddicombe – headspace.com, 23. Amit Ray – knowyourquotes.com, 24. Emily Fletcher – audible.co.uk, 25. Csikszentmihalyi, M (1992) Flow, 26. Brolin, C (2017) In the Zone, 27. 'The Holiday' (film 2006), 28. The Khan Academy – khanacademy.org, 29. Vanderbilt, T (2021) Beginners, 30. Edwards, B (2012) Drawing on the Right Side of the Brain, 31. Gelb, M J (1995) Lessons from the Art of Juggling, 32. Waitzkin, J (2007) The Art of Learning, 33. Ludwig Wittgenstein – quora.com, 34. Jackson-Brown, H (2012) Life's Little Instruction Book, 35. Nelson Mandela – goodreads.com, 36. Seligman, M (1990) Learned Optimism, 37. Huffington, A (2016) The Sleep Revolution, 38. Cameron, J (1993) The Artist's Way & (2021) The Listening Path, 39. Moore, S J (2016) Why Eating Less and Exercising More Makes You Fat, 40. Gallup Global Wellbeing Survey 2010 – gallup.com, 41. Anders Erickson – nytimes.com, 42. Laszlo Polgar – en.wikipedia.org, 43. 'King Richard' (film 2021), 44. Richardson, J (2009) Dream On, 45. Duhigg, C (2012) The Power of Habit

Looking Outwards

Understanding our world & our place in it

The last two chapters have examined the contents of our history and explored some possible components of our future. The past is a done deal, banked experience - although we do have the option to reframe it if we so desire. The future holds unlimited potential with the possibility of pursuing untrodden paths. The past provides a context for the present and the future offers new ways of being and doing. The horizontal past-future axis of the model has a chronological dimension that locates us in both time and space.

The vertical axis is the focus of the next two chapters. Chapter 3 is looking upwards and outwards – our understanding of the wider world and our place in it. Chapter 4 reverses the telescope and focuses inwards – an exploration of how we see ourselves. We can slide up and down this vertical axis, looking outwards and inwards according to the demands of the situation. This pair of chapters adds to the insights of the first two chapters and provides additional context to our understanding of *The Now* elaborated in Chapter 5.

The old conundrum - which came first, the chicken or the egg? Is understanding the world a precursor to understanding ourselves, or is it the other way round, when we understand ourselves, we are better placed to understand the world? I have chosen to look outwards first simply because people are social animals and have difficulty living in isolation.

> *The global community of the kibbutz changed my world perspective. It was a different echo chamber. I also learned how to speak Hebrew. Those two years changed me.*
>
> *I am an internationalist by outlook. I am also a patriot. I'm passionate about finding out about the world.*

I recently attended a lecture by John McCarthy[1] who was taken hostage by Islamic Jihadists in Beirut and was initially held in solitary confinement. Later he shared a cell with Brian Keenan. McCarthy's experiences reinforced the significance of social interaction and the genetically imprinted need for human relationships.

The notion of people being programmed to be social beings is not a new one. The idiom that *No man is an island* is taken from a 1642 sermon by the Dean of St Paul's Cathedral, John Donne.[2] Although Donne is regarded as one of the greatest English poets, it is ironic that this famous quotation was from a sermon and not a poem. Here is the full quotation:

> **"No man is an island entire of itself; every man is a piece of the continent, a part of the main; if a clod be washed away by the sea, Europe is the less, as well as if a promontory were, as well as any manner of friends or of thine own were, any man's death diminishes me, because I am involved in mankind. And therefore, never send to know for whom the bell tolls; for it tolls for thee."[2]**

John Donne and John McCarthy, in very different ways, both underscore the importance of human connection and its significance in the wellbeing and survival of the individual. Death is the earthly severing of human connection and is the final frontier for 'whom the bell tolls'. Coming to terms with our own mortality is a recurring theme of life and a social challenge to be embraced. Bereavement highlights the importance of social connection and provides a stark reminder that we are indeed social animals.

My first written assignment as a trainee teacher required me to answer the question *Are children primarily shaped by their nature or nurture?* Which is more influential, our genetic endowment or our environment? My simplistic answer was that they both have a part to play, and they interact with one another. The ability to use DNA to understand who we are and to predict who we will become has moved on dramatically during the intervening years, but the nature – nurture debate still rages!

The DNA revolution and genomics has made DNA personal by giving us the power to predict our psychological strengths and weaknesses from birth. "This is a game-changer that will have far reaching implications for psychology, for society and for each and every one of us."[3] The DNA fortune teller is the culmination of a century of genetic research investigating what makes us who we are.

You are born with your outlook on life. The downside of being an optimist is that you are regularly disappointed. Being a pessimist means living with a cloud over your head.

When psychology emerged as a science in the early 20th Century, it focused on the environmental causes of behaviour. Environmentalism — the view that we are what we learn — dominated psychology for decades from Freud onwards, the family environment, or nurture, was assumed to be the key factor in determining who we are. In the 1960s, geneticists began to challenge this view. Psychological traits from mental illness to mental abilities clearly recur in families, but there was a gradual recognition that family resemblance could be due to nature or genetics rather than nurture alone, because children are 50 per cent similar genetically to their parents.

Since the 1960s, scientists conducting long term studies on special relatives, like twins and adoptees, have built a mountain of evidence showing that genetics contributes importantly to psychological differences between us. The genetic contribution is not just statistically significant, it is massive. Genetics is the most important factor shaping who we are. It explains more of the psychological differences between us than everything else put together.

The most important environmental factors, such as our families and schools, account for less than 5 per cent of the differences between us once we control for the impact of genetics. Genetics accounts for 50 per cent of psychological differences — not just for mental health and school achievement, but for all psychological traits, from personality to mental abilities.

I was brought up as a Catholic and suffer from Catholic guilt. My parents did not have very high expectations for me. They hoped I would get married and have children. They had very different expectations for my brother.

This research does underscore tangentially the importance of the environment — genetics accounts for only half of the psychological differences between us, so where does the other 50 per cent emanate from? For most of the 20th century environmental factors were thought to be overwhelmingly important in determining who we will become. Genetic research shows that this is not true. In fact, the environment makes siblings reared in the same family as different as siblings reared in separate families. Family resemblances are due to our DNA rather than to our shared experience, such as supportive parenting or growing up in a broken home. What makes us different environmentally are random experiences, not systematic forces like families. The implications of this finding are enormous. Such experiences affect us, but their effects do not last; after these environmental bumps we bounce back to our genetic trajectory. Indeed, what looks like systematic long lasting environmental effects are often reflections of genetic effects.

Robert Plomin[3] believes that the DNA differences inherited from our parents at conception are the lifelong source of psychological individuality, the blueprint that makes us who we are. A blueprint is a plan. DNA isn't all that matters but it matters more than everything else put together in terms of the psychological traits that shape us. These inherited DNA differences are the blueprint for our individuality and do not change during our lives.

Emerging scientific research provides us with the ability to disentangle our genes and the environment. The focus on the importance of inherited DNA is likely to attract criticism for resurrecting the nature versus nurture debate. Let me leave the final word to Plomin. "Throughout my career I have emphasised nature and nurture, not nature versus nurture, by which I mean that both genes and environment contribute to the psychological differences between people. Recognition that both genes and the environment are important fosters research at the interplay between nature and nurture, a very productive area of study." [3]

You will have your own sense of how you have been shaped by the interplay of your genetic inheritance and the lived experiences of your unique history. Chapter 1 raised these reflections to the conscious level. I continue to be fascinated by the interplay of nature and nurture, both as a parent and as an educator. We all construct our own homespun theories of child and adult development, not least as parents and particularly as grandparent! A cursory overview of the history of development theory provides an interesting context for some of the recurring themes identified in this book.

So, how do we get to understand the wider world and our place in it? I have chosen to summarise five influential theories and I invite you to use this section as a basis for interrogating your own view of development. I will summarise each theory and present them in approximate historical order – from the oldest to the most recent. You may find some of the theory tedious but stick with it and reflect on the implications for your own past, present, and future development.

Freud's Psychosexual Development Theory[4]

Sigmund Freud was one of the most influential thinkers of the early 1900s. While constructing an approach to psychoanalysis, Freud also developed a psychosexual development theory. In it he proposed that the personality of a child moves through five psychosexual stages. During each stage, sexual energy (libido) is expressed in a different way and through different parts of the body.

In contrast to geneticists, Freud proposed that a child's experiences (nurture) dictate personality and behaviour patterns in adult life. Thus, early life experiences have a huge impact on later development. The five distinct stages are:

The oral stage (birth to 1 year)

During the oral stages the libido is centred in the baby's mouth. The baby puts various objects in its mouth to satisfy the libido, and thus its id demands. Life is characterised as being oral, or mouth oriented. Behaviours such as sucking, biting, and breastfeeding are taken to be proof of this contention. We see evidence of adult oral personalities in smokers, nail biters, finger chewers and thumb suckers when they are under stress.

The anal stage (1 to 3 years)

The libido becomes focused on the anus and great pleasure is derived from defecating. The child is now fully aware that they are a person, and that their wishes can bring them into conflict with the demands of the outside world, notably their caregivers. Freud believed that this type of conflict comes to a head in toilet training, when restrictions are imposed on when and where the child can defecate. The nature of this first conflict with authority can determine the child's future relationship with all forms of authority.

Early or harsh toilet training can lead to the formation of an anal-retentive personality who hates mess, is obsessively tidy, punctual, and respectful of authority. This is deemed to be related to the pleasure derived from holding onto their faeces when toddlers. Not as daft as it sounds. The anal explosive on the other hand, is the product of a liberal toilet training regime. An adult anal explosive is the person who wants to share things. They like giving things away and can be messy, disorganised, and rebellious.

The phallic stage (3 to 6 years)

This is when the child's libido (desire) centres upon their genitalia. The child becomes aware of anatomical sex differences, which sets in motion the conflict between erotic attraction, resentment, rivalry, jealousy, and fear. Freud called this the *Oedipus Complex* in boys and the *Electra Complex* in girls. He suggested that these complexes are resolved by the child adopting the characteristics of the same sex parent.

The latency stage (6 years to puberty)

The libido is dormant and no further psychosexual development takes place. Freud thought that sexual impulses are repressed during this stage and that sexual energy is sublimated towards school, hobbies, and friendships. Much of the child's energy is channelled into developing new skills and acquiring new knowledge.

The genital stage (puberty to adult)

The genital stage begins in puberty. It is a time of adolescent sexual experimentation that leads to settling down and the living with another adult in our 20s. Freud believed sexual instinct is directed to heterosexual pleasure and heterosexual intercourse. Fixation and conflict may prevent this, with the consequence that what he deemed sexual perversions may develop.

Another layer to Freud's theory is the development of the **id, ego**, and **superego**. He believed that the id is instinctual and primitive. It is something we are born with and the mechanism that controls our sexual drives. The id is often seen as unrealistic and impulsive.

The ego develops during the first few years of life and represents reality. Freud believed that the ego is responsible for decision-making and reason.

The superego develops during the phallic stage and is the source of morality. Our morals, according to Freud, are learned from our parents or other caregivers. Since the superego is meant to control the id and ego, it attempts to calm down the id's desires, while also helping the ego recognise morals-based goals. Likewise, the superego can be thought of as our conscience. It is what makes us feel guilty when we do something wrong and rewards us when we do something right.

Arguably Freud's theory is highly unscientific and yet has influenced thinking for over a hundred years. Do our values, moral compass, and ways of seeing the world come from our significant caregivers? Does his psychosexual theory provide a lens for you to examine your own development? If behaviour really is a function of experience, what childhood experiences have shaped your thinking and ways of being now?

Piaget's Cognitive Development Theory[5]

Published in the mid-1950s, Piaget's *Cognitive Theory* suggested that children think differently to adults - a revolutionary perspective at the time. The belief that a child's cognitive development is tied to developmental milestones has proved to be a pervasive educational theory and one that is still alive and well today! In essence, this theory divides the child's life into four separate stages.

Sensorimotor stage (Birth to two years)

Infants progressively construct knowledge and understanding of the world by relating their experiences of seeing and hearing to the objects they interact with, through grasping, sucking, or moving. They progress from reflexive actions at birth, to the beginning of symbolic thought towards the end of the stage. It has been interesting watching our latest grandchild move through this stage.

Children learn that they are separate from the environment. **Object permanence** is one of their most important accomplishments. Object permanence is a child's understanding that an object continues to exist even though they cannot see or hear it. Peek-a-boo is a game in which a child who has not yet fully developed object permanence responds to the sudden hiding and revealing of a face. I watched a parent playing this game in the supermarket this morning. By the end of the sensorimotor period, children will quickly lose interest in peek-a-boo, so make the most of it while you can.

Preoperational stage (2 to 7 years)

Piaget delineated this second stage by observing sequences of play. This stage starts when the child learns to speak. During the preoperational stage, Piaget noted that children do not yet understand concrete logic and cannot mentally manipulate information. Play involves pretending and yet the child has trouble seeing things from different points of view. (Some adults still do.)

The pre-operational stage is thin in terms of mental operations. The child forms stable concepts as well as magical beliefs. The child is not able to perform operations mentally, only physically, (hence the name of the stage). Thinking at this stage is still egocentric and the child has difficulty seeing the viewpoint of others.

Concrete operational stage (7 to 11 years)

Logic and thought process are becoming more mature. The child begins solving problems. Abstract hypothetical thought has not yet developed, and so the child can only solve problems that draw on concrete events or objects.

Inductive reasoning begins to emerge, drawing inferences from observations to make a generalisation. In contrast, children struggle with deductive reasoning, using a generalised principle to try to predict the outcome of an event.

The two significant processes in this stage are the development of logic and the elimination of egocentrism. The child acquires the ability to view things from another person's perspective, even if they think it is an incorrect one! However, problems can only be solved by applying logic to concrete objects or events, and not to abstract concepts or hypothetical tasks.

Formal operational stage (age 12 and upwards)

The adolescent's verbal problem solving ability develops. Thinking becomes more scientific - options can be tested and problems solved. Hypothetical-deductive reasoning develops, and the concepts love, logic, and values can be understood. The future holds a myriad of fascinating possibilities – the emergence of **possibility thinking**. (See Chapter 2.)

Cognitive changes are developing during this stage, particularly in the way adolescents think about social issues and their place in the world. Self-consciousness is heightened and uniqueness and invincibility come to the fore. The adolescent's egocentrism can be divided into imaginary audience and personal fable.

Imaginary audience involves the belief that others are watching and are interested in the things we do. The impact of social media is interesting in this context. Personal fable consists of believing you are exceptional or unique in some way. Again, social media has a significant part to play.

So, what has Piaget got to offer us? My understanding of Piaget's theories is that each stage is marked by a specific developmental goal. Early years educators often have an acute understanding of how the young child learns and the importance of developmental goals. In summary, each stage is marked by a specific developmental goal:

In the sensorimotor stage, the goal is **object permanence** — the ability to understand that an out of sight object still exists.

The goal of the preoperational stage is **symbolic thought** — the ability to use symbols and images.

In the concrete operational stage, the goal is for the child to develop **logical thinking** — the ability to solve problems in a more scientific fashion.

The formal operational stage produces the development of **abstract thinking** — the ability to think through alternative hypotheses.

Parents, grandparents, and caregivers, as well as educators, can use Piaget's theories to support their child's development. From the perspective of this book, I believe it is helpful to understand that cognitive development and the quality of our thinking is an active process from the beginning to the end of life. Intellectual growth is possible at any age and stage. We can use our unique history and the ideas of others as lenses to understand what is going on in our lives now. Infants learn that new objects can be grabbed in the same way as familiar objects, mature adults learn that new perspectives can be added to our cognitive repertoire. How exciting is that!

Erikson's Psychosocial Development Theory[6]

Erikson's model of psychosocial growth replaced Freud's controversial theory centred on psychosexual development. Erikson's work shifted the focus, based on the eight-stage framework he constructed.

Stage 1: Trust versus mistrust (Birth to 18 months)

During the first months of life, we are uncertain about the world and seek to develop trust in the people around us. We are reliant on our caregivers for warmth, love, stability, and nurturing. If these things are reliable and predictable, we gain confidence and a sense of security.

If care is inconsistent and unreliable, then mistrust will develop. The baby could become anxious and start to believe we can have little or no control over our environment.

Stage 2: Autonomy versus shame and doubt (18 months to 3 years)

The infant begins to develop a heightened sense of personal control and acquire feelings of independence. Children become increasingly mobile and mature physically. According to Erikson, toilet training is crucial in learning physical control and the development of autonomy. Success in managing bodily functions (see Freud above) leads to a sense of personal power and feelings of autonomy.

By contrast, toilet accidents can lead to a sense of shame and doubt. An appropriate balance between autonomy and shame and doubt is essential to later psychosocial development.

Stage 3: Initiative versus guilt (3 years to 5 years)

During these pre-school years, there is conflict between initiative and guilt. We learn to assert ourselves in social interactions. To some adults, this behaviour may seem too assertive or even aggressive and yet interpersonal skills are simply being rehearsed.

Excessive adult restrictions and/or criticism can foster a sense of guilt in the child. Success in Stage 3 leads to feeling confident about using our initiative. Is the right balance between initiative and guilt a key to developing a positive mindset in later life?

Stage 4: Industry versus inferiority (5 years to 12 years)

By now we are immersed in the world of education. Teachers play a significant role in this stage, while peer groups and social interactions are also increasingly relevant. Winning approval is a motivating factor, and we learn to associate it with displaying competencies valued by our peers and significant adults.

Learning how to handle these social situations and academic expectations is the key challenge and failure to manage successfully can result in a sense of inferiority. Learning to fail, however, can also be a crucial element in our maturation, leading to increased motivation. A point the triathlete Alistair Brownlee explores in his book 'Relentless'.[7]

Stage 5: Identity versus confusion (12 years to 18 years)

These years can be daunting to both adolescents and their parents. They provide an opportunity for teenagers to explore some of the themes raised in the first two chapters of this book – such as beliefs, goals, and values. This also is a period of searching for personal identity and a more mature sense of self. Teenagers become increasingly independent and begin to consider higher education, careers, family, peers, and wider social issues.

It is vital for young adults to learn the roles they could adopt as they mature. Body image and sexuality are important parts of this process. Success leads to clarity about identity. Inability to create a sense of identity and clarity about our place within society can lead to confusion. Ultimately identity provides an integrated sense of self that will last throughout our lives, guiding how we behave and what we believe.

Stage 6: Intimacy versus isolation (18 years to 44 years)

The intimacy versus isolation conflict occurs around age 30. At this point, role confusion is ending. In the early part of this stage (the first 10 years or so), young adults are still eager to fit in with friends and peers. Erikson believed that intimacy can be isolating and at the same time can generate anxiety about partners ending a relationship.

Once people have established their identities, they are ready to make long-term commitments to others. They can form intimate, reciprocal relationships and can make the sacrifices and compromises necessary to maintain such relationships. If people cannot form intimate relationships, a sense of isolation may result.

Stage 7: Generativity versus stagnation (45 to 64 years)

Generativity involves concern for guiding the next generation. During middle age, the primary development task involves contributing to family, friends, and the wider society. This leads to a feeling of productivity and accomplishment. In contrast, a person who is self-centred (ego-centric to use Freud's terminology) and is unable or unwilling to contribute to society can develop feelings of stagnation, based on a lack of productivity.

Stage 8: Integrity versus despair (late adulthood, 65 years and above)

The societal expectation is that people will retire and relax in late adulthood and that leisure activities and family will assume higher priority. There is time to reflect on the meaning of life, pursue leisure activities, and invest in health wealth. Where health allows, there is the opportunity to become more autonomous.

This stage provides opportunities for retrospection. Feelings of contentment accrue to those who feel they have led a happy and productive life. Despair pursues those who see only disappointment and unachieved goals. More of this later.

Erikson's theories have been criticised as simplistic and prescriptive, nevertheless they provide an interesting template for both reflection and future planning. Take time to reflect upon what the pairs of words that characterise each stage mean for you:

> » trust v mistrust
>
> » autonomy v shame
>
> » initiative v guilt
>
> » industry v inferiority
>
> » identity v confusion
>
> » intimacy v isolation
>
> » generativity v stagnation
>
> » integrity v despair

What resonance do these words have for you? When you look back through Erikson's stages in your own life what do you notice? Where would you like to put your future focus?

Bowlby's Attachment Theory[8]

John Bowlby's work shaped my early thinking on child development. He asserted that development is based on the child's innate need to form attachments. These attachments may involve people, places, or things.

Bowlby, like Freud, was a psychoanalyst and he placed great emphasis on how early childhood experiences shape later mental health. His theory is rooted in evolutionary psychology. He believed that humans, like other animals, are biologically predisposed to form attachments to survive. The research demonstrated that infants separated from their parents will usually react in one of three ways upon being reunited.

Secure attachment: these infants showed distress upon separation but were easily comforted when their parents returned.

Anxious-resistant attachment: these infants experienced greater levels of distress and upon reunion seemed to both seek comfort and to seek to punish the parents for abandoning them.

Avoidant attachment: these infants displayed little stress upon separation and at reunion either ignored or actively avoided their parents.

It seems obvious that a child's attachment style is largely a function of the caregiving received in her or his early years. Those who received support and love from their caregivers are more likely to be secure, while those who experienced inconsistency or negligence are more likely to be anxious in later life. Bowlby's theory suggests that infants construct a working model based on the relationship they have had with their primary caregivers. This model helps them understand themselves, other people, and the wider world.

Bandura's Social Learning Theory[9]

Albert Bandura was quite different to other learning theorists who looked at learning as the direct result of conditioning, reinforcement, and punishment. He asserted that most human behaviour is learned through observation, imitation, and modelling. He also believed that the modelling we do of others is not limited to behaviour, but also includes attitudes and emotional responses. In this way, his theory embraces both cognitive and environmental factors.

Modelling is a simple process. Children notice how their parents, caregivers and other significant figures behave and encode that information. Later in life, people replicate the behaviour they have seen modelled in childhood (and in adult mentors and role models). Bandura built his theory on the foundation of classical and operant conditioning. Simply, when a child exhibits a behaviour that has been encoded from a model and that behaviour is rewarded, the child is more likely to repeat it. When a caregiver applauds a desirable behaviour, the child is reinforced by that positive reward. Conversely, when a child's behaviour is met with a negative consequence, they are less likely to repeat the behaviour.

My captain at boys' brigade and my pastor were real role models to me, as was my GP trainer.

Bandura broke from the straitjacket of fundamental behaviourism by suggesting that the environment is just one determinant of learning and behaviour. Indeed, he suggested that our intrinsic motivations and even our current mental state have much to do with how we learn and behave.

The utility of research theories and perspectives

These five theories provide us with a range of working models to help us unpack how we got to be where we are today. In broad terms, psychosexual and cognitive theories look inside, whereas psychosocial, attachment and social learning theories focus on our interactions with others. My suggestion is not to write off these theories as deterministic or simplistic, but rather to view them as alternative perspectives to help us make sense of the world - much like the fable of the six blind people and the elephant. They are all exploring a different part of the elephant – different perspectives on the same thing.

We cannot go back and rewrite our earlier life, although we may choose to frame our significant experiences in a different way. What we can do is embrace the future possibilities the world holds for us.

Let me add two less well-known models to your *perspective bank*.

Firstly, in one of my earlier books, *Living a coaching lifestyle*, I provided a thought starter conceptualising my life from 0 to 100 years. The model has five 20-year stages.

For me, Stage 1 revolved around family and education. I have vivid memories of sporting events, both playing and watching. Examinations also loom large at transition points. What are your memories?

Stage 1	0-20 years	Rapid physical and mental growth
Stage 2	20-40 years	Early career and early family stage
Stage 3	41-60 years	Maturing career and maturing parent stage
Stage 4	61-80 years	Opportunity zone and clarifying stage
Stage 5	81-100 years	Inner world and final preparation stage

Table 2 Life concept in 5 stages

Stage 2 was about marriage, parenthood and increasing workplace responsibilities. It was also about my spiritual awakening and exploration of faith.

Both my parents died during Stage 3, and I began to realise no one is immortal. My children grew up and left home and this stage was characterised by enormous change, both personally and professionally. I discovered more about what I wanted to do.

I am now in Stage 4 and seeking to maximise the possibilities that it provides. Being clear about my purpose shapes the way I spend my time - faith, family, and intellectual growth.

Stage 5 beckons and I suspect will focus heavily on my inner world – the focus of Chapter 4. This stage is more about chipping away the debris rather than acquiring more stuff!

In his book *From strength to strength*, Arthur C Brooks[10] describes the ancient Indian teaching that a proper life must be lived in four stages, called 'ashramas'. Each ashrama lasts approximately 25 years.

Ashrama 1 is the period of youth and young adulthood and is dedicated to learning.

Ashrama 2 is where a person builds a career, accumulates wealth, and builds a family. (This sounds straightforward, but Hindu philosophers identify some of life's most common traps inherent in this stage. People become too attached to earthly rewards like money, power, sex, and prestige.)

Ashrama 3 is where we purposefully begin to pull back from work and become more interested in spirituality and deep wisdom.

Ashrama 4 stage comes in older age and is dedicated to the fruits of enlightenment. The goal of the last phase is to drink from the chalice of life's deepest secrets.

You may or may not find the ages and stages approach helpful. We are not obliged to take on theories and models without questioning them.

I believe it is useful to reflect on how we believe our genetic inheritance and past life have shaped us and caused us to interact with the world in the way we do.

My early family life has made me wary of relationships and attachments. I don't want to be let down!

The interplay of our nature and nurture is a fascinating one. Life is constantly changing and evolving, and we have future stages to explore. How will you choose to shape your future and live every day of your life to the full?

People as social animals

People are social animals and are designed for relationship. The examples I elucidated earlier, John Donne and John McCarthy, illustrate this contention. As you reflect on your own life what do you notice about the ways in which you interact with other people? What does your current social network look like?

I suggest you draw a **socio-gram** to represent the people you interact with. A socio-gram is a graphic representation of our social linkages — the network of the people we interact with directly. It is explained in Exercise 6 at the end of this chapter.

Alternatively, you may prefer to construct a **social circles diagram**. This is another way of charting your significant social contacts. This is Exercise 7 at the end of the chapter.

The Oxford Dictionary's definition of a **friend** is "a person with whom one enjoys mutual affection and regard". The same dictionary defines **acquaintance** as "a person one knows slightly". The likelihood is that you spend more time and energy on the people close to you on your sociogram and people that populate the inner circles of your social circles diagram. This seems obvious, but sometimes there are surprises. Most friends probably start as acquaintances.

I have three or four close friends and I am friendly with 30 or so people. I have loads of acquaintances, probably over 100.

My close friends are influential, they are encouraging, supportive and provide new insights.

I value family, friends, and relationships.

Jim Rohn[11] suggests the five people we spend the most time with have the greatest influence upon us, and vice-versa. Tony Buzan[12] terms this your 'mastermind group'. Who is in your mastermind group and how does their influence shape your view of the world?

I believe it is possible to have a negative mastermind group.

Bandura (see earlier in the chapter) suggested that most human behaviour is learned through observation, imitation, and modelling. He also believed that the modelling we do of others is not limited to behaviour, but also includes attitudes and emotional responses. Have a close look at your mastermind group and your two inner circles on the model. Are there recurring themes in the way they interact with you? How do people gain entry to our mastermind group and inner circles?

The structure of this book and indeed life, locates the NOW between your past and your future. The psychological theories and stages of life models I have elaborated earlier in this chapter provide insights into how we have become who we are today and where we might like to go next in a conscious way. I imagine Freud, Piaget, Erikson, Bowlby, Bandura, and numerous others laboured long and hard to shed light on human development. None of these people know the intimate details of your unique history or future aspirations – you are the expert in your own life! My key message is that you have an infinite number of choices, and you are in control of the choices you make.

I am an eternal optimist and see opportunities over the horizon.

Behaviour is a function of experience and conscious choice, although we are often programmed to make decisions at the unconscious level. A myriad of influences conspire to create our worldview and day-to-day priorities. Financial crises, international conflicts and word-wide pandemics cast a long shadow over our lives. One of my interviewees highlighted the importance of controlling what you can control, influencing what you can influence and relaxing about the rest. Is this possible? You decide!

Let's pause and reflect on what we can control, what we can influence what we have absolutely no impact upon. The only person I can control is myself and that might be an illusion. We are shaped by our genetics and our history – our caregivers, families, schools, role models, and social networks. We live in a particular milieu – our worldview is shaped by national and international events mediated through newspapers, television, and social media. We are social animals influenced by the people we spend time with. How do we make sense of it all? In the words of Mary Poppins, "Let's start at the very beginning, it's a very good place to start." When I look outwards, what do I choose to focus upon? The world has dealt us a hand of cards, we decide how to play them!

The choices we make are influenced by our history, stage of life, the people we interact with and local, national, and international considerations. And numerous other things! As a Stage 4 or Ashrama 3 person, I have established some criteria to inform my choices. I will summarise my 'expert in my own life' thinking as a challenge for you to do the same.

What and who are the priorities in my world? (See Exercise 5 earlier)

> » My faith and my God
> » My family
> » My friends
> » My work
> » My society – local, national, and international

As I look outwards and upwards, God is at the heart of everything – my creator, my guide, and my saviour. My family are also pivotal and my second priority – my wife, my children, and my grandchildren. Close friends also occupy a high priority and overlap with my church community and family. Work in the widest sense gives shape and meaning to my life. I choose to coach, to write, to read, and to grow intellectually. Society is a much more slippery and distant concept for me. I am polite to my neighbours, I support good causes, I put my bins out on time and I vote in local and national elections. I watch the news, check Twitter, read my on-line newspaper and I ask myself 'How much influence do I have?' Perhaps the better question is 'How much influence do these things have on me?'

In the latter part of this chapter, I invite you to reflect on how you constructed your current view of the world – both the process and the outcome. From conception to this very moment, you have been building your worldview. The psychological theories and stages models outlined earlier provide a framework. My framework may be very different to yours as we look through the spectacles of our unique history. Behaviour is shaped by experience – how has yours been crafted in the crucible of life?

When you look outwards and upwards, what do you see?

Your learning began in the womb and can continue to the moment of death. As you navigated your way through Freud's **oral stage** or Piaget's **sensorimotor stage** how and what did you learn? Our five senses enable us to experience the world around us: sight, hearing, smell, taste, and touch. These developing senses are taken for granted in the maturation process and attain greater significance by their absence, such as blindness or deafness.

Sight: the eyes capture light and convert it into images for the brain to process. Sight enables us to see the size, form, colour, and location of the things that are in our environment. Bandura's social learning theory suggests that learning comes from direct experience and sight provides a medium for registering what is around us. Sight plays a crucial role in emotional intelligence and the ability to read others' body language. Sight is also the vehicle that creates awe and wonder when we see a glorious sunset, stunning scenery, or the face of a loved one.

Hearing: the ears tune into the sounds that are around us. These sounds are communicated to the brain and provide a range of messages about danger, love, the environment around us, and a myriad of other things. Young children quickly recognise the voice of their caregivers, and we all have favourite voices we like to hear. Music is a source of great joy for many, and most people love to engage in conversation (theirs and others). Indeed, I would contend that listening is an indicator of emotional generosity.

Smell: the nose provides the brain with messages about the world, based on the nature of the smell. This sense allows us to distinguish between different aromas – simplistically pleasant and unpleasant smells. Pleasant smells stimulate the appetite, create a sense of wellbeing, or give us positive feelings about another person. Unpleasant smells have the opposite effect and may signal danger in relation to rotting food, dangerous chemicals, or unwashed people.

Taste: the tongue communicates taste to the brain, signalling both danger and delight. This sense enables us to access the flavour of things, such as food and drink. When I hear 'salty', I associate the word with nuts or crisps, while 'sweet and sour' conjures up both Chinese food and Scotch whisky. One unfortunate aftermath of Covid-19 is the absence of taste and the realisation of what an important part taste plays in the enjoyment of our daily lives.

Touch: the skin provides us with the ability to experience the sense of touch. This sense allows us to feel how something is and to know its texture, its hardness, and its temperature. The skin is the largest organ of our body and a much more significant source of information to the brain than we realise. 'Loving touch' is a significant element of healthy development – children hugged by their parents or adults embraced by their loved ones.

Child development and adult consciousness are mediated through the five senses. An expanding range of stimuli are registered and communicated to the clearing house that is the brain. I love libraries (and book shops) and our brain is constantly purchasing more books for its ever-expanding library. Some books are weightier, some more colourful, some more frightening, but they all add to the contents of the library. In this metaphor, you are the librarian, and you can choose which books to take off the shelves. I have chosen six tomes I would like to bring to your attention in the rest of this chapter and they are: listening, questioning, observing, reading, researching, and reflecting.

Listening

My most popular offering on Twitter goes like this: "We show the quality of our care for people by the way we listen to them." This is a direct quote from a former colleague Barbara Ward who helped me understand the enormous power of listening. God designed us with two ears and one mouth for a reason, so that we can do twice as much listening as speaking. Not everybody we meet seems to be aware of this!

> *I listen well and I am very curious. I have always listened very carefully, and I remember conversations, including things not being said as well as what was said. Listening is an important skill.*

Some expectant mothers play soothing music to their unborn baby in the womb. Sounds increasingly fill the world of the neonate – parent(s), siblings, television, music and so on. Playgroup or nursery school provide another set of soundscapes and so it goes on. Why do children from musical families love music – is it part of the soundtrack of their early lives? More importantly what are significant people saying to the child as they move through the variously named developmental stages? How soon does the child develop their own unique form of self-talk?

Listening is a vital life skill; it is pivotal in how we conceptualise the world. We spend a large part of our waking hours engaged in the business of listening, either to others or to ourselves. The quality of our listening ebbs and flows for a variety of reasons, such as tiredness, the quality of the message, or the nature of the topic. As we look outwards and upwards, we make conscious and unconscious decisions about what to listen to and what deserves our 'best listening'. The notion of applying different levels of listening provides a useful working model.

Level 1 listening is superficial and does not require a significant investment of energy. Often this is just ambient noise, although random sounds related to safety or opportunity may trigger a higher level of attention.

Level 2 listening involves a greater sense that this information might be important. Formal and informal teaching beget this level. The listener is mentally registering and recording what may be useful later. A crude definition of learning.

Level 3 moves us on to a deeper level that involves both empathy and the ability to see things through another's eyes. What Piaget designates as the formal operational stage. This level requires more 'work' and willingness to engage on the part of the listener.

Level 4 goes beyond the normal and is difficult to define, involving both intuition and sensitivity. In my world view this could be seen as listening below the surface or as listening to the guidance of the Holy Spirit.

Listening accesses some of the building bricks we can use to make sense of the world. It provides the basis for systematic reflection and possibility thinking to flourish. Julia Cameron's book *The Listening Path*[13] deconstructs the listening process in a helpful way. Four of her chapter headings provide entry points to the listening process:

» Listening to Our Environment

» Listening to Others

» Listening to Our Higher Self

» Listening to Silence

Superimpose those four headings over the earlier theories and models and evaluate the impact of the listening you have done in your life so far. The young child listens to their immediate environment and receives messages from caregivers, siblings, and significant others. The mature adult can choose what 'others' to listen to – their mastermind group, their political leaders, their heroes. We are constantly sifting and refining hard and soft information to support or challenge our world view. A theme I will explore in more detail later is the impact of what we hear when we listen to ourselves – the quality of our self-talk. I believe managing the nature of this self-talk is fundamental to our success.

Listening to silence is a rare activity for me. Some of you may be accomplished meditators or mystics. This is a potential growth point, and I am interested in exploring meditation and the ability to still the restless mind during Stage 5 or Ashrama 4 in my future life. *How accomplished is your listening?*

Questioning

"You can tell whether a man is clever by his answers. You can tell whether a man is wise by his questions."[14] I am certain the Nobel Prize winner Naguib Mahfouz was using 'man' in a generic sense to encompass child, woman, and man – all ages and stages. We listen to understand and make sense of the world. We ask questions to short circuit our learning and understanding. Incessant questioning characterises the stage Piaget defines as 'preoperational' – where, what, how? Young children are asking questions to understand the world and their place in it. As we grow and mature our questioning may become more sophisticated, but we are wrestling with the same challenge, not least because our existence is constantly changing as we move from Life Stage 1 to Life Stage 5. Nothing stays the same and different life stages generate different questions, both practical and philosophical.

"The art and science of asking questions is the source of all knowledge."[15] Asking the right question at the right moment often provides the key to unlocking a complex situation. Questions help us find answers and encourage our interlocutor to speak. Often the greatest challenge in academic study is to refine your research question. What is your current research question and who are you asking? Self-coaching is a useful practice, particularly when you ask yourself the 'right' questions. You may be undertaking self-coaching formally or informally, in the shower, in the car, or in your reflective learning journal.

Questions should have a starring role in the personal development process. As a coach and a developer of coaches, I believe questions have a powerful role to play in navigating life. Classrooms are awash with teacher questions, both 'closed' and 'open'. Young children have an insatiable desire to learn and helping them pose the right questions expedites and illuminates the learning process. Teenagers, in what Erikson describes as Stage 5, grapple with questions about their own identity and place in the world. Greta Thunberg has touched a nerve by highlighting questions about the significance of climate change and the impact upon our collective future. Further down Erikson's model, in Stage 8 people have time to frame questions about the meaning of their life and their priorities for this stage. Retrospection generates learning about both personal and collective triumphs and disasters. What can I pass on to future generations in my family and wider society as a modern elder? What questions can I pose for them to short circuit their life learning?

Observing

Observations are rarely neutral or objective. You might challenge this bold contention if you are a professionally trained observer. My experience indicates that our observations are rarely made in a vacuum. We are the product of the interplay of our genes and our socialisation and therefore we are looking from a particular perspective. The blind person who had the elephant's tail had a very different sense of the animal to the one holding the trunk! As a lapsed Ofsted Inspector, I suggest that people interpret the same Standard Framework differently. We are wedded to looking from our own perspective.

Classroom observation should be an objective process, as should selection interviews, and yet our focus is drawn to our own interests and prejudices. The comments of spectators at a live sporting event, such as soccer or tennis, illustrate that observers see the same event differently. Some sociologists take the view that there is no such thing as objective truth, simply shared subjectivity – reality is a social construction.

"To acquire knowledge, one must study, but to acquire wisdom, one must observe."[16] People watching is a popular pastime and as I have already suggested some people make a living out of it. Professionals observe and interpret events on behalf of others – political commentators, sports journalists, Ofsted Inspectors to name but a few. The observation should precede the interpretation. The notion of *halo* or *horns* applies equally in selection interviews and everyday social interaction. We like something about someone and endow them with a halo and seek evidence to support this positive appraisal. Horns engender a search for the negative.

I enjoy listening and watching people.

We construct our version of reality using our five senses, but this is not an objective process. Our observations are mediated through the lens of our experience. I go to Specsavers every couple of years for an eye test and to purchase a new prescription for glasses. I have choices about which pair to purchase. The new pair of glasses helps me see more clearly and to access smaller print. Are you aware of the prejudices and biases that colour your ways of looking? Are you in need of an eye test to expedite your acquisition of wisdom?

Reading

Reading is a fundamental life skill. It provides a window on the world and an entry into the lives of others. Learning to read is a rite of passage and a key to unlock future learning. The teaching of reading, like many other strands of early education, has been influenced by both solid research and the latest fads and fancies. I don't remember how I learned to read, whether it was a 'phonic' approach or the 'look and say' method. What I do remember is that my father was a voracious reader and usually consumed eight books a week. Undoubtedly Bandura would say he was my role model and my passion for reading is the result of his modelled behaviour.

As an educator I am fascinated by the fact that some adults are avid readers and others have not opened a book since they left school. We will all have our own views on how to get children, and adults, to read. My belief is that it is important to find the right material and medium to inspire the desire, whether a physical book or an on-line offering. Nothing breeds success like success. Provide children with inspiring reading material and appropriate encouragement and they will become successful readers. Unfortunately, it is a little more complicated than that!

If you are reading this book, it is almost certain that you are a successful reader. How did you get to be successful? Possible reasons quickly come to mind – effective teaching, a book-rich environment, encouragement from significant others, the right books for your age and stage, and so the list goes on. Most children can bark at print, but a passion for reading is a different animal. Reading has instrumental value in making sense of the world – the ability to read instructions and road signs for example. A passion for reading has a different texture – the joy of deliberate learning or the willing suspension of reality in a novel. Fiction and non-fiction are both strands of the same glorious process.

Groucho Marx made a very instructive quip. "I find television very educating. Every time somebody turns on the set, I go into another room and read a book."[17] Reading requires time and focus, whether it is reading for learning or reading for pleasure. The learning/pleasure dichotomy is probably a false one anyway. What is significant is the motivation to read. To write this book, I have read a wide range of literature and I am acutely aware of the computer jargon – GI/GO – garbage in, garbage out! The selection of authors I have read is both opportunistic and a reflection of my interests. Motivation is the key!

"Think before you speak. Read before you think."[18] This is excellent advice. As you look outward and upwards, how is your view of the world informed by your reading? I use 'reading' in a generic sense to encapsulate fiction and non-fiction - books, magazines, newsletters, social media and so on. The printed word in any form! I post on and read Twitter – a reflection of my age and stage. My teenage granddaughter accesses different platforms and is impacted by different 'influencers' and 'social disruptors'. When you review your own reading choices what do you notice?

Researching

Life is a research project. Freud wrote from a psychosexual perspective, while Erikson chose a psychosocial approach. Bowlby's attachment theory and Piaget's cognitive development work shaped my views as a teacher and most probably as a parent. I could argue that my views of the world are research informed. This may or may not be true! As a grandparent, I have a whole host of child rearing strategies at my disposal, some of them research-based, others experience-based and yet others prejudice-based.

We are the expert in our own life. We construct theories about how the world works and they inform our behaviour. The development of these theories begins at birth and ends at death. Our research has both formal and informal components, ranging from deliberate learning to chance experiences. We learn from observation, reflect on the data, and decide whether to apply this learning to future behavioural choices. Some of us are more acute observers than others, some more reflective, and some quicker learners!

The dictionary defines research as "the systematic investigation into the study of materials, sources, etc., in order to establish facts and reach new conclusions." As children move through various development stages, they are constantly establishing facts and reaching new conclusions. As adults we can decide to become lifelong learners and embrace new experiences, in the style of Josh Waitzkin and Tom Vanderbilt profiled in Chapter 2. Research provides the gateway to new learning.

As part of my MA, I studied a research methods module and the insights gained opened a much wider range of future studies. Research methods and perspectives are many and varied, as the early part of this chapter illustrates. Crudely they can be divided into objective and subjective. It is much the same with our own lifestyle development theories – some are based on hard facts and others on feelings and prejudices. Take a moment to reflect on how you have developed your own theories of life.

Reflecting

In my view reflection is a growth activity that merits some priority in our allocation of time and energy. Many of my interviewees expressed a similar view.

I am comfortable with reflection, I have always been analytical, reflective, and taking the time to do it.

Leadership development programmes often require participants to keep a reflective learning log that charts significant moments in their learning. The action of writing things down brings them to your attention and gives you the opportunity to decide how those insights will inform your future behaviour. It is a way of analysing what is going on around you. It also provides data to help us understand how we see as we look outwards and upwards.

Julia Cameron[13] suggests three longhand A4 daily pages. This is free writing that downloads your current stream of consciousness. It is both cathartic and revealing. As I read back through my 'daily pages', I can see recurring themes. This ethnographic approach is rich in personal insights and well worth the time invested. Some people enjoy writing, while others prefer speaking. Coaching involves verbal reflection. As the client articulates their thinking, patterns emerge, and the skilful coach can help people make sense of these patterns and design appropriate action. The written and the verbal are not mutually exclusive as one informs the other.

Samuel Pepys and Anne Frank are famous diarists and exponents of systematic reflection. Diary writing is a variant on the reflective learning log. Both my father and my father-in-law kept diaries that I read after their deaths. Some of the entries were especially poignant and usually involved the family. (There must be a significant learning point there!) Journaling is another version of recording significant learning in your life. In my two earlier books, I have encouraged readers to keep a journal to chart their thinking. It may even grow into your life story.

I started to keep a journal two years ago and it helps me clarify the life I want and to appreciate what I do have.

Bruce Feiler opens his wonderful book *Life is in the Transitions*[19] with an account of his father's attempted suicide on being diagnosed with Parkinson's Disease. Feiler's response was to ask his father questions about his childhood that eventually led to Mr Feiler Senior authoring a 65000-word book – his life story. As an aside, the title captures an essential truth, life is in the transitions. (See the exercise at the end of Chapter 1). The sub-title of the book — *Mastering Change at any Age* — provides an imperative for action and leads us to look inwards, the focus of Chapter 4.

Exercise 6 My Sociogram

A sociogram is a visual representation of your relationships, either personal or professional. It highlights communication within a defined group and indicates distance, nearness, conflicts, co-operation, and the structure of subgroups.

For example, approximately 450 adults attend the same church as me and unsurprisingly I do not have the same amount of contact with each one. There will be some people my wife and I have regular contact with, such as other leaders, people in the same small group, or colleagues discharging the same ministry. There will be others we chat with infrequently at church events, and still others we have never spoken with.

A sociogram is not a picture of objective reality, but rather a subjective representation of a social network. A sociogram is not static, it changes over time as people join or leave the defined group. Indeed, it is a convenient method of charting social change.

Take a sheet of plain A3 paper. Put yourself in the middle of the paper and define the border of the group you are representing.

Place significant others on the sheet according to your own criteria, such as:

* Frequency of contact
* Social nearness
* Social distance
* The sub-group they are part of
* Role

Populate your own sociogram with the names of the people involved. Reflect on the picture that emerges. Where would you like to make changes? What specific actions do you plan to take? And so on.

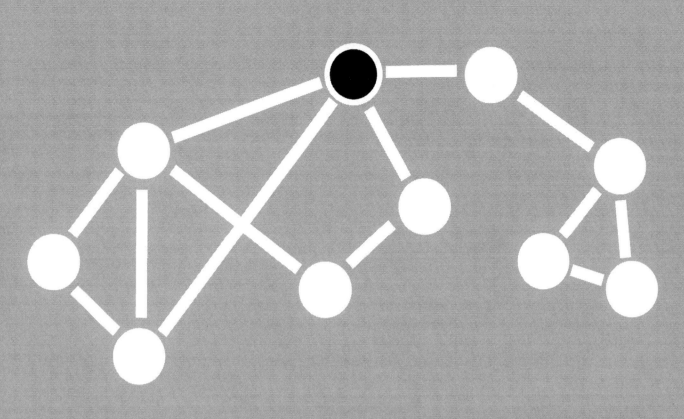

Figure 6 Socio gram of your interpersonal relationships

Exercise 7 My Social Circles

This is another way of charting your significant social contacts. Again, put yourself in the middle of a piece of paper and draw a series of concentric circles around yourself.

Choose the number of circles and the criteria for allocation to each one. As an example, I have designated four concentric circles in my model:

* Circle 1, at the centre of the diagram, specifies the people closest to me – partner, children, parents, and siblings.

* Circle 2, the next circle out, might contain your wider family and close friends.

* Circle 3 could chart less-close friends, work colleagues and regular ac- quaintances.

* Circle 4 is a catch-all for all the other people in your social network – casual relationships and people you meet infrequently.

Over time people may move in and out of circles as social relationships change and develop. Have fun with this exercise and involve others in refining it.

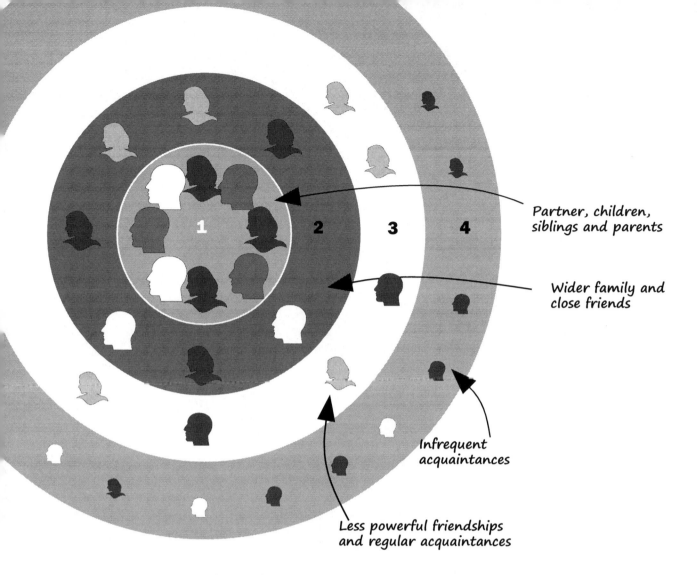

Partner, children, siblings and parents

Wider family and close friends

Infrequent acquaintances

Less powerful friendships and regular acquaintances

Figure 7 Social circles of your interpersonal relationships

Bibliography

1. John McCarthy – Lecture in London June 2022, 2. John Donne – Sermon at St Paul's Cathedral 1642, 3. Plomin, R (2018) Blueprint, 4. Freud, S (1905) Three Essays on the Theory of Sexuality, 5. Piaget, J (1977) The Essential Piaget, 6. Scheck, S (2005) The Stages of Psychosocial Development According to Erik H Erikson, 7. Brownlee, A (2021) Relentless, 8. Bowlby, J (1953) Childcare and the Growth of Love, 9. Bandura, A (1977) Social Learning Theory, 10. Brooks, A C (2022) From Strength to Strength, 11. Rohn, J (2011) My Philosophy for Successful Living, 12. Buzan, T (2007) Grass Roots Leaders, 13. Cameron, J (2021) The Listening Path, 14. Naguib Mahfouz – brainyquote.com, 15. Thomas Berger – universallifetools.com, 16. Marilyn vos Savant – brainyquote.com, 17. Groucho Marx – bookroo.co, 18. Fran Lebowitz – goodreads.com,19. Feiler, B (2020) Life is in the Transitions

Looking Inwards

The beginning of all wisdom

Aristotle captured the essence of this chapter in eight words: "Knowing yourself is the beginning of all wisdom."[1] We can choose to look outwards at the world as we did in Chapter 3, and we can reverse the telescope as Aristotle suggests and look inwards.

I have the capacity to be able to think more deeply and more clearly. The ability to look inwards.

Looking outwards and inwards is not an either/or choice, rather one perspective informs the other. We seek to make sense of the world and who we are in it. This is complicated — the world is constantly changing and so are we. To hold either or both still to examine the detail could be seen as an artificial construct. Let's have a go anyway!

The self-concept develops through the early years of our lives and continues to be modified till death. As I rehearsed in the last chapter, Freud, Piaget, and Erickson, employed an 'ages and stages' approach. By contrast, Bowlby and Bandura employed an 'environmentalism' approach focusing on social interactions. The dictionary definition reflects this dualism. "Self-concept: an idea of the self, constructed from the beliefs one holds about oneself and the response of others."

As you age and learn who you are, you discover what is important to you. These self-perceptions become more detailed and organised as you mature. At its most basic, self-concept is a collection of beliefs you hold about yourself, shaped by the response of others. The concept of the 'looking-glass self' suggests that we learn who we are from the reactions and responses of others. Most of this happens at the unconscious level. Self-concept then is a cognitive or descriptive component of who we are.

Self-concept is a portmanteau term that captures how we perceive our own behaviours, abilities, and unique characteristics – what makes us who we are! Self-perception generates how we feel about the person we feel we are, whether we are competent or incompetent in particular ways. It is reasonable to assume that the self-concept is more malleable early in life and that as we grow and mature our self-perceptions become more detailed and organised. Nevertheless, I would strongly resist the temptation to fall into determinism and I believe we still have agency and choice at any stage of life.

Carl Rogers[2] suggested that our self-concept comprises three component parts.

The ideal self: The person we aspire to be. This person has the attributes and qualities we desire. This is our perfect self. Chapter 2 explored the future self we would like to grow into.

Self-image: How we see ourselves now. Our self-image is made up of multiple component parts, such as our physical characteristics, personality traits, and social roles. Our unique history has shaped how we see ourselves now.

Self-esteem: How much we like, accept and value ourselves. Multiple factors affect our self-esteem – including how others see us, how we compare ourselves to others, and the roles we play in society. This can shift and change according to feelings and circumstances.

Self-concept is not always congruent with perceived reality. If there is a mismatch between your self-image and your ideal self, your self-esteem can be impacted negatively. Rogers called this phenomenon *incongruence* and suggested it had its earliest roots in childhood. When children are obliged to earn their parents' love through expected behaviours and levels of performance and fail, they begin to experience low self-esteem. Unconditional love and encouragement on the other hand, foster *congruence* where the three parts Rogers identified are in harmony.

> *I recognised the power of encouragement. And I regret that I wasn't encouraged more as a child. Encouragement is about reminding people what they are good at.*

One of the most powerful pieces of educational research I have encountered highlighted the importance of self-concept. *Pygmalion in the Classroom* authored by Rosenthal and Jacobson[3] demonstrated that teacher expectations have a dramatic impact on pupil self-image and self-esteem, leading to starkly different performance outcomes. Teachers were given false information about the previous ability of their students – children were labelled falsely as 'able' and 'not able'. At the end of the academic year, the children performed in line with the expectations of their teacher and very differently to the previous year. The power of the self-fulfilling prophecy!

Thus, self-concept develops at least in part through our interactions with others. I ask you again: Who is in your mastermind group? What expectations of you are they manifesting? What deliberate and accidental feedback are they giving you? Your unique history and the influences of significant others have made you who you are today. The great news is that you can choose to modify elements of your self-concept. It is not cast in stone!

We are not yet two pages into this chapter, and you may be beginning to feel that this focus on the self is pure indulgence. There may be an element of truth in this perception and yet… I contend that we need to understand self before we can fully understand others. Indeed, a more extreme view could be that it is altruistic to spend time reflecting on why we behave as we do to enhance our interactions with others. Go with the flow for the rest of the chapter.

> *Self-confidence can mutate into regrettable arrogance, and I am very aware of that.*

This 'inner' work leads to better 'outer' interactions. Suspend your judgements for now. There are many and varied ways of looking inwards. I encourage you to undertake a period of mental self-examination, adopting a scientific approach to this enterprise. I will present you with a series of pegs to hang your thinking on and the rest is up to you. My chosen pegs recur in the literature and in the responses of my interviewees. Conceptualising your brain as a changing room with rows of pegs to organise your thinking is a useful metaphor that captures my approach to the rest of this chapter.

Peg 1: Self-talk

Our most frequent talk partner is ourselves. It is estimated that we spend more than 90% of our waking hours talking to ourselves. This internal dialogue takes place both when we are alone and when we are interacting with others. It is the running commentary on our lives, the thoughts and beliefs that bounce around in our head and then inform our behavioural choices. It is the soundtrack to our lives. We are shaped by what we say to ourselves – our self-concept reflects what we have heard. Stated simply, the nature of our self-talk has a profound effect on the quality of our existence.

Self-talk comes in two basic varieties – negative and positive. Negative self-talk is largely destructive, and it generates pessimism and low self-esteem. By contrast, positive self-talk predisposes us to success, and it generates optimism and possibility thinking. We have a degree of control over what we say to ourselves, just as we can choose what we say to others. How do you choose to speak to yourself and what is the nature of the recurring self-talk scripts you run in your head and speak out of your mouth?

I am very action focused and I always try to think of the positive in every situation.

Invest in listening to your self-talk scripts in a conscious and deliberate way. Record what you are hearing in your journal and reflect upon the impact these scripts are having (see Exercise 8 at the end of this chapter). Which recurring scripts are hampering you and which ones are serving you? These scripts emanate from your habitual thinking and the prevailing image you hold of yourself. It is believed that we each have approximately fifty thousand thoughts every day. It would be impossible to capture every thought, but I am suggesting that you identify the strong recurring themes that feature in your inner dialogue.

Nursery children verbalise their thinking as they are playing. We can listen in on their self-talk and hear their thinking. As we mature this becomes internal dialogue with an audience of one – ourselves. Self-talk is your mental evaluation of what you have done, what you are doing now and what you will do next. It has past, present, and future components. Each internal conversation has a potential impact on our self-concept and in turn future behavioural choices. In fact, it could be argued that our actions and outcomes in life are a direct reflection of the quality of our self-talk. "Words matter. And the words that matter most are the ones you say to yourself."[4]

I think you can choose to change!

Newsflash from one of my interviewees - you can choose to change your self-talk. I believe it is eminently helpful to reduce the percentage of negative self-talk and to increase the percentage of positive self-talk. If you are wedded to mental self-flagellation, reducing negative self-talk is not a good strategy. On the other hand, if you want to be healthier, happier, and fun to be around, then more positive self-talk is the way forward!

The self-talk cycle has four component parts:

  » What we say to ourselves

  » The impact on our self-image

Figure 8 The self–talk cycle

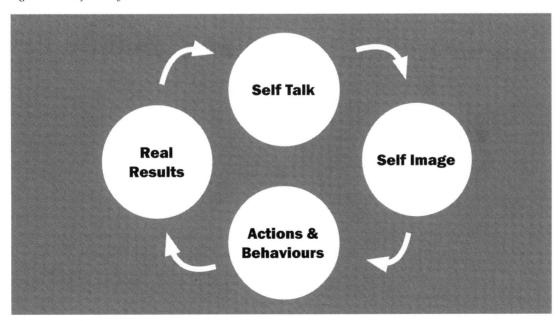

» The resulting actions and behaviours

» The real results generated

The obvious place to break into this cycle is to review the nature of our self-talk. What is the balance of negative and positive self-talk? We can choose to shift the balance by consciously decreasing the negative and increasing the positive. It will be almost impossible to eradicate negative self-talk completely – like weeds in the garden, negative thoughts will continue to pop up from time to time. It is possible, however, to weed the garden and to give the seeds of positivity a better chance of flourishing. Louise Hay suggests a way forward: "I monitor my self-talk, making sure it is uplifting and supportive to myself and others."[5]

She makes the interesting observation that the nature of our self-talk will have an impact on others, notably the people we live with, the people we work with, and the people we socialise with. Our 'actions and behaviours' will generate 'real results' in these relationships. So, investing in our self-image could have an altruistic component. It is axiomatic that the person who will be impacted most by the quality of our self-talk is ourselves.

Shad Helmstetter, who authored the delightfully entitled book *What to say when you talk to your self*[6], believes that there are five separate levels of self-talk. They are summarised in Table 3.

Here is an example of the five levels using healthy eating as the topic:

Level 1: "**I can't** stop eating unhealthy and fattening food."

Level 2: "**I should** stop eating unhealthy and fattening food as I am becoming overweight."

Level 3: "**I never** eat unhealthy and fattening food and **I no longer** put it in my mouth."

Level 4: "**I am** a healthy eater and I enjoy feeling slim and fit."

Level 5: "**It is** a joy to eat in the way we are designed to eat."

The first three levels are doomed to failure and will encourage unhealthy eating. The unconscious mind does not understand negatives and simply registers unhealthy and fattening food. You have programmed yourself to see it and to eat it. Levels 4 and 5 both focus on the positive and programme the unconscious mind to eat healthy food. "I am a healthy eater and I enjoy feeling slim and fit" has the following characteristics:

Table 3 Listening Levels (after Helmstetter)

Level	Listening quality	Description
1	The level of negative acceptance "I CAN'T..."	The subconscious mind is listening and acts on negative instructions.
2	The level of recognition and need to change "I SHOULD..."	This level is beguiling: it looks as if it should work, but actually works against us. It creates guilt and disappointment.
3	The level of decision to change "I NEVER...I NO LONGER..."	Remember your subconscious will believe anything if you tell it long enough and strongly enough.
4	The level of better you "I AM..."	This is the most effective self-talk we can ever use.
5	The level of universal affirmation "IT IS..."	This is the self-talk of oneness with God, a unity of spirit which transcends all worldly things and gives meaning to our life.

» It is first person, singular – I

» It is present tense – this is what I do now

» It is active – I have agency

» It is positive – it highlights the benefits.

Identify an area of your habitual negative self-talk you would like to change. Reframe it in a way that is first person, present tense, active, and positive. I find writing down a new positive script (an affirmation) helpful. Write the words and read them over, close your eyes and see the picture the words create, and then feel the emotions that will accrue from taking the action. In short:

» Write the words

» See the picture

» Feel the emotions.

Consciously affirm the new script every day for a month and it will move from the conscious level to the unconscious level – you take the action without thinking. *Dubin's Dichotomies* is a model that summarises the process.

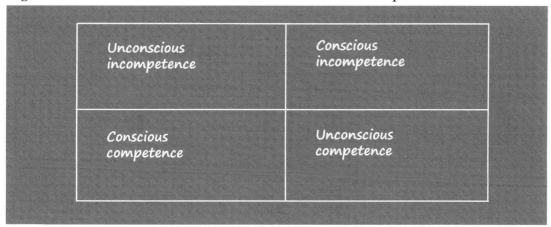

Figure 9 Dubin's Dichotomies

At the **unconscious incompetence** stage, we may be unaware of the power of our self- talk. New learning helps us to realise that negative self-talk is destructive and unhelpful, and we can recognise what is going wrong – we have now moved into **conscious incompetence**. We seek to replace habitual negative self-talk with new, positive scripts, and move into **conscious competence**. Usually within a month the new script will be lodged in our unconscious mind, and we will act without conscious thought - we are now in a state of **unconscious competence**.

Start listening to both what you say to yourself and to what you say to others. Phrases like *I could never do that, I never get things right, I cannot do that at my age* are obvious examples of negative self-talk. I play golf with a range of people of varying abilities, and I have noticed that the better golfers rarely engage in negative self-talk. The less successful golfers are experts in rehearsing negative scripts like, *I will miss this, Why am I so useless?, I am the unluckiest golfer in the world.* If they are saying these things for others to hear, what are they saying to themselves?

At a very different level of sporting excellence, Alistair Brownlee cites the example of Cathy Freeman preparing for the Olympic 400m Final in Sydney to highlight the importance of self-talk. She was the Australian poster athlete with the expectations of a nation weighing on her shoulders. In Brownlee's view, a brain scan in the couple of hours before the race would have revealed her inner preparation. "Freeman's brain activity, drawing on every ounce of experience, the silencing of internal voices, **the self-talk**, the management of crushing pressure, must have been immense, before you get to the athletic performance itself."[7] She won the gold medal!

The notion of silencing internal voices is a powerful one. Negative self-talk will pop up and in its most extreme form manifests itself as impostor syndrome. "I don't know what I am doing, and it is only a matter of time before everyone finds out" is classic impostor syndrome self-talk. Even my most sophisticated and professionally successful coachees manifest impostor syndrome tendencies.

I do experience impostor syndrome, although I am getting better at it.

Psychotherapy is helping me move from comfort to courage and let the impostor syndrome voice out!

Impostor syndrome could be seen as positive as it reduces the likelihood of complacency and arrogance. It is all a question of balance. To restate my view, our challenge is to reduce negative self-talk and at the same time increase positive self-talk.

Positive self-talk is simply choosing to talk to yourself in a way that inspires and encourages you. "Relentless, repetitive self-talk is what changes our self-image."[8] Yesterday I noticed when I was 'running' up a very steep hill (I was overtaken by a couple of athletic snails) the difference between saying to myself "I can do it" and "I am enjoying doing it". The first self-talk snippet suggests there is the possibility of failure, while the second statement leaves no room for equivocation and celebrates success!

I frequently receive notifications of software updates for my telephone and computers, and I always take the time to install them. I am inspired by the consequences of not doing so. The analogy is a simple one, the brain is the computer and self-talk is the software programme. Self-talk is the software that drives our internal computer. Does yours need a regular upgrade?

Peg 2: Storytelling

The dictionary defines a story as "an account of imaginary or past experiences, a narrative or tale." Self-talk over the course of our life builds our unique story – our life story. Chapter 1 illuminated our past experiences and Chapter 2 identified the experiences we desire in the future. These are the stories we tell ourselves and others and most importantly we are the storyteller. As a continuation of the exploration of the quality of your self-talk, I invite you to listen to the life story you tell yourself and others.

The *narrative approach* probably started life as a way of sharing oral history around the stone age campfire and has enjoyed many iterations ever since. In the last century it was adopted as a therapeutic approach within psychiatry and has recently become another strand in the toolkit of coaches and other helping professionals. Storytelling has both reflective and self-revealing elements and it helps us make sense of our own lives.

The *National Storytelling Network*[9] is a community of practitioners operating in the United States and Canada and it suggests that there are five key elements to storytelling. I will use these as a framework to communicate the significance of storytelling.

Storytelling is interactive

The interactive nature of our storytelling suggests a two-way interaction between the storyteller and one or more listeners. We are the primary listener to our own story. We know our historical story and we may choose to share parts of the narrative with others. Responses to the story shape further actions and our story continues to unfold until the moment of death. The way we frame the past, present, and future story is highly significant.

Storytelling uses words

The nature of the words we use to tell our story is critical. Self-talk is made up of words and these are the same words we use to tell our story to ourselves and others. The words may be negative, neutral, or positive. Individual words may have a particular meaning for us. The key issue is that we get to choose the words. What do you notice about the words you choose?

Storytelling uses actions

The self-talk cycle summarises how words beget action. Our words shape our self-image, which in turn influences our actions and behaviours and the results become part of our life story. I am stretching the Network's model to make a different point and I acknowledge the editorial liberty I am taking. Their meaning involves the way we tell the story, employing vocalization, physical movement, and gesture. Our bodies tell our life story before we even open our mouth.

Storytelling presents a story

Autobiography is a distinct genre of literature and most of us are fascinated by the lives of others. We can choose to read autobiographies or listen to speakers talking about their own story. I contend we have no choice but to listen to our own emerging life story every day of our lives. This is our inner dialogue as we negotiate with ourselves as storyteller. This is an interactive process, and we have agency in choosing our own text.

Storytelling encourages the active imagination of listeners

In storytelling the listener imagines the story and is transported to another place. As we tell ourselves our own life story it has past, future, and present components. The past has factual elements. The future contains hopes and aspirations. And the present is where the real action is taking place. I am encouraging all of us to unleash our active imaginations.

My passion for storytelling was engendered by my father's evocative tales of his experiences in the Second World War. Although these tales were highly sanitized, his skill as a storyteller sucked me in. As a parent, teacher, and presenter, I seek to tell stories that will resonate with my audience. It is only recently that I have realised the power of the stories I tell myself. The stories I construct for an audience of one. The penny dropped when I was reading a light-hearted account of Elise Downing's 5000-mile run around the coast of mainland Britain.

On one particularly challenging day she writes "I started to wonder: how much we are just a story we tell ourselves."[10] Her book is entitled *Coasting* and the subtlety of this title captures where she was in her life story. She asserts that a long run, in this case 5000 miles, gives you a lot of time for self-reflection. Looking inwards is the focus of this chapter and I am relieved to realise that the 5000-mile run is not the only mechanism for self-reflection. She concludes her rumination by saying "It's not easy to change the stories we tell ourselves, but I need to start trying."

I think this is a helpful aspiration for us all – not to change the stories that are serving us, but to modify or forget the ones that are hampering us. Beliefs about ourselves and others may change over time, while our values remain constant. In Chapters 1 and 2, we explored **values** at some length. My core values have not changed and are unlikely to do so – they are integrity, wisdom, serenity, and authenticity. When you analyse your own core values what do you see and how do they inform your story telling?

I aspire to act with **integrity** in every situation. When I don't succeed, cognitive dissonance is generated, and I experience a level of discomfort. The behaviour does not match my guiding script. My choice is to modify the behaviour and to maintain the underlying value of integrity. The story I tell myself is instrumental in doing this. The story shapes the behaviour.

God gave King Solomon the choice of any gift[11] and Solomon chose **wisdom**. What an excellent choice! All our actions and behaviours are the result of our thinking. As the years pass and our bank of experiences grows, the benefit should be that our wisdom increases. The pursuit of wisdom drives the desire to learn, and this value underpins my story as a life-long learner.

Serenity is a value I aspire to rather than have fully achieved (more in the next chapter). A new chapter of my story needs to be written. It is on my *to do* list.

Authenticity is a key behavioural driver and the narrative I share with myself is that I generally act accordingly. These four values are an important foundation for my life script and inform my storytelling. They provide guidance, parameters, and a way of conceptualising my inner world.

Part of the skill of the successful storyteller is to choose the right words. As I suggested earlier in this chapter, successful self-talk scripts have four characteristics - first person, present tense, active and positive. We are the central character in our script. The past and future elements of our life story are supporting acts to what is happening on stage now. Crucially, the story is a positive one and words chosen should reflect that positivity.

Barbara Fredrickson has written a book on that very subject, aptly entitled *Positivity*. She describes the content of her book as ground-breaking research on how to release your inner optimist. "We all know negativity; it looms large and is easy to spot. Negativity pervades your self-talk and your judgements."[11] Fredrickson suggests increasing our positivity quotient and elaborates six reasons for doing so:

> » Positivity feels good
>
> » Positivity changes how your mind works
>
> » Positivity transforms your future
>
> » Positivity puts the brakes on negativity
>
> » Positivity obeys a tipping point
>
> » You can increase your positivity.

I suggest the way to increase your positivity is to include more positive words in your story. Listen to your own life story (see Exercise 9 later). Focus on the words you are using – what is the current balance of negative, neutral, and positive words? Start small and decide to change the ratios – decrease negativity and increase positivity. Neutral words are unlikely to capture the interest of the listener! In short, choose your words carefully.

Indulge me by engaging in a short exercise to illustrate the point. Without thinking about it, identify five positive words. My immediate five are: *optimism, success, happiness, love,* and *health.* Same guidance, identify five negative words: *pessimism, failure, unhappiness, loneliness,* and *illness.* Speak out the two lists with a gap in between – how does each list make you feel?

It is impossible to eradicate negativity completely and it is also undesirable. We need to be negative about injustice, famine, abuse and so on. The tenor of my message is to shift the balance of positivity and negativity. Fredrickson suggests a ratio of 3:1 in favour of positivity. Words are the building blocks of thought and carry enormous power. We underestimate their impact at our peril.

"If we understood the power of our thoughts, we would guard them more closely. If we understood the awesome power of our words, we would prefer silence to almost anything negative. In our thoughts and words, we create our weaknesses and our strengths. Our limitations and joys begin in our hearts. We can always replace negative with positive."[12]

My final thought on storytelling is inspired by the *Wheel of Life* (Exercise 5 at the end of Chapter 2). Our life story is made up of lots of sub-stories. The exercise invited you to identify the six to eight spokes on your wheel – such as: spiritual, family, learning/developmental, social, professional, health/fitness, financial, and sport/hobbies. Each of these spokes has its own story that is developing and changing.

We can choose to act in any of these areas and re-write parts of our story. For example, my financial sub-story has been modified by changes in my professional career and my sport/hobbies narrative has changed in relation to my health/fitness levels. All the sub-stories are interlinked and act upon one another. Together they make up our life story.

As the storyteller, we choose the content, the words, and the way the story is told to ourselves and others. Some stories move us forward and some hold us back, choose the ones that are interesting and exciting and generate positive action. "Stories are our nearest and dearest way of understanding our lives and finding our way onward."[13]

Peg 3: Possibility Thinking

The next phase of your life is replete with possibilities – opportunities, challenges, triumphs, and disasters. You are both the navigator and the pilot. You decide how to play the hand of cards you are dealt. At the simplest level, possibility thinking is willingness to see opportunities rather than limitations. It is a mindset that keeps the reticular activating system permanently open for business, searching your environment for new challenges and opportunities.

I would love to change the world!

This bold aspiration emanates from the belief that it is possible to make a difference, regardless of our age and stage. Often the greatest opportunities are right under our nose, as the famous 'acres of diamonds' story I recounted in my first book illustrates. Two years ago, few people thought many of us could work from home, conducting our business on-line using *Zoom* or *Teams*. Yet here we are implementing home and hybrid working. I used to be agnostic about online banking and now my financial world is challenged by the internet going down for one hour. Ten years ago, we had no inkling of the simplicity of *Apple Pay*! And so, it goes on.

Remember if you always do what you have always done, you will always get what you have always got. Maximising possibilities involves new ways of thinking. One of my favourite writers, Thomas Merton[14], captures the essence of this approach to life. "You do not need to know precisely what is happening, or exactly where it is all going. What you need is to recognise the possibilities and challenges offered by the present moment, and embrace them with courage, faith, and hope."

We can choose to dwell in possibility as we look inwards, as well as when we look outwards. I am writing this part of the book at harvesttime, and this is an apposite metaphor to help us recognise where we are in our lives. The seeds have been planted and nurtured and now is the time to bring in the harvest. As the grandson of a farmer, I have always loved this season of the year – the buzz and excitement of harvesting and the promise of harvest festival celebrations ahead.

Possibility thinking involves both positive self-talk and creative storytelling. Indeed, possibility thinking is a portmanteau concept that draws together many of the themes criss-crossing this book and our lives. For example, a 'growth mindset' is a way of seeing the world through a lens of curiosity, a place where opportunity and challenge combine to provide new possibilities. Throw off the restrictions of a 'fixed mindset' and explore the diamonds beneath your feet.

I choose to push out of my comfort zone and recognise exciting possibilities.

I am very aware of limiting beliefs.

These interviewees and several others demonstrated a willingness to embrace new ways of being and to adopt a possibility mindset. One recurring theme in the interviews was the significance of health issues, both our own and those of people close to us. These occurrences provide unwanted possibilities and highlight that we do not live in a Pollyanna world of pink gingham and rocking chairs. We do not know what challenges tomorrow will bring, but we can be certain there will be some.

Bruce Feiler, in his excellent book *Life is in the Transitions*[15], terms these unwanted possibilities such as a health issues, financial shocks, or divorce as 'disruptors'. He suggests that the average person can expect around 36 disruptors in their adult life. That is an average of one every year to eighteen months! So, it is sensible to improve how we navigate them. Like big red buses, you may not see any for a while and then two or three come along together. Feiler calls these unwanted episodes of overlapping disruptors 'life-quakes'. Several disruptors may take place concurrently or one major bomb may explode into our lives and cause the quake.

A life-quake is a potentially devastating experience that can disorientate and destabilise us. Feiler's research suggests that we may go through three to five of these massive reorientations in adult life. Life-quakes may be voluntary or involuntary, but either way we must learn how to navigate them. My wife has developed her role as a bereavement listener following the life-quake of her own mother's death. A positive response to a devastating experience.

Possibility thinking acknowledges that transitions are coming as sure as night follows day. How we navigate these transitions has very little to do with age and stage and is much more about how we choose to respond to vicissitudes and challenges. As you look inwards what do you see in terms of your own resilience and ability to cope? As you reflect on your life story, what reliance muscles have you developed and what coping skills are in your toolbox for life?

One benefit of growing older and reviewing your life story is that you can see and recognise emerging patterns. We cannot be sure what is going to happen tomorrow. We can, however, learn from what has happened in the past and we can use that learning to inform our present decision making. More on that theme in Chapter 5. The challenge is to get the balance right — embrace future opportunities, while acknowledging that we are not God and cannot control everything.

Possibility thinking is a conscious choice that requires awareness and determination. I prefer to focus on the positive aspects of possibility thinking while acknowledging that unwanted things will happen. The challenge is to figure out how to evolve and rewire us for the next part of our lives. Andrew Scott and Linda Gratton extol the possibilities of *The New Long Life*[16] and conceptualise the twin themes of longevity and technological change. The linear life is dead, and the future holds the possibility of a more fluid, multi-stage existence with breaks in between.

For obvious reasons, I am drawn to authors who celebrate that we are the architects of our own destiny. We can choose to challenge the shackles of ageism and throw off negative self-fulfilling prophecies about later life. It is noteworthy that in a world beset with financial and social challenges, the wisdom of older people is one of the few increasing natural resources. Chip Conley[17] emphasises the importance of wisdom in the workplace and uses his own experiences to illustrate how to embrace the unexpected possibilities later life offers.

Possibility thinking encapsulates both the peaks and valleys of life. A life well-lived embraces all the experiences that come our way, both the positive and negative ones. Our challenge is to learn from these experiences and to increase our road worthiness. We may even be able to help others negotiate the challenges on their road, not by telling them what to do, but by helping them navigate. That is what inspired me to set up our Family Learning Community. "Who you are tomorrow begins with what you do today."[18]

Peg 4: Feedback and Reflection

Cicero asserted many centuries ago that "It is not by muscle, speed, or physical dexterity that great things are achieved, but by reflection, force of character, and judgement."[19] Regardless of age or stage, we all enjoy receiving positive feedback. This is both encouraging and life-affirming. Negative feedback is a different kettle of fish – its usefulness depends on the way it is delivered and who it is delivered by. Once again, I am slightly misquoting Eleanor Roosevelt, but the essence of what she said is "I reserve the right to ignore feedback from people whose judgement I do not respect".[20]

The Merriam-Webster Dictionary defines feedback as "the transmission of evaluative or corrective information about an action, event, or process to the original or controlling source."[21] This evaluative information can range across a continuum from highly positive to highly negative, with various degrees of each along the way. Corrective information can be delivered to improve performance or express disappointment. As suggested above, the usefulness of the feedback depends on how it is delivered, by whom, and at what point.

The delivery is one part of the process, the recipient's response and subsequent action is another. I asked my interviewees two interrelated questions (questions seven and eight in the interview schedule) concerning reflection and feedback, they were as follows.

How do you manage reflection as a development activity?

How do you respond to feedback and criticism?

The rocket fuel of evaluation appears to be feedback, either from others or from self. The first two pegs – self-talk and storytelling – can be viewed as a form of reflection. Cicero emphasised the utility of reflection centuries ago and this approach has been endorsed by a myriad of observers ever since. In the 1960s reflection as a personal growth strategy came to the fore and it was further popularised by *reflective practice* in healthcare settings in the 1980s.

As a personal and professional growth strategy it appears to be here to stay. In its simplest form, 'reflective practice' is the ability to reflect upon your actions and engage in a process of continuous learning. For nurses and midwives, it is a prescribed activity to fulfil the requirements of revalidation. For each of us it could be argued that self-revalidation takes place in an informal way almost daily. I would like to quote in full the response of one interviewee to question 7.

As I have got older, I have got better at reflection. I ask myself 'How did that go?' or 'How could I have done that better?' Reflection is something we should all do to think about ourselves critically. You can teach people to be more reflective by showing them the benefits. It does require a level of self-criticism.

It was only when I reviewed this interview that I realised the richness of these insights. Allow me to deconstruct the thinking:

» I have got better at reflection as I have got older

» I ask myself reflective and evaluative questions

» The power of reflecting critically is recognised

» It is possible to be taught to do it well

» The benefits justify the investment of time and energy

» The process requires a level of self-criticism.

It is noteworthy that *critically* and *self-criticism* are used in a positive sense. Thinking critically is framed as a scientific way rather than as a manifestation of negative self-talk. Self-criticism is seen as a growth activity. By way of context, this individual has worked in a range of professions and she has engaged in a wide range of personal and professional learning experiences. Do the above responses to the question reflect this varied professional background or have they simply revealed an innate ability to reflect critically?

The same interviewee answered question eight in an equally thoughtful fashion.

The usefulness of feedback depends on how it is delivered. It is helpful when it is constructive and developmental. I am a sensitive soul, and I can engage in lengthy rumination. I go over and over the same situation. Negative feedback takes me out of my comfort zone. I can't just brush it off!

My deconstruction of this answer highlights several other themes:

» The utility of feedback is influenced by how it is delivered

» Most of us prefer constructive and developmental feedback

» Reflection and rumination are different activities – the former is positive, and the latter feels negative

» Rumination involves revisiting the same territory again and again

» Negative feedback generates discomfort

» It is difficult to 'brush off' negative feedback.

It is entirely possible that I am overlaying my own thinking to the responses of this interviewee. To provide balance, I have reviewed the answers of other interviewees to this pair of questions. Here is a random sample of answers, starting with responses on reflection:

I am a reflector and a talker. I work it out in therapy sessions.

I engage in contemplation and review. It is often analysis – 'What went well?' 'What was the impact?'

I am naturally reflective, although I tend to overthink things. When in doubt, I check it out with others.

The answers to the feedback question tend to be defensive:

I have found the space inside myself where I don't care.

Negative feedback hurts me deeply.

I have learned to keep quiet and take feedback and criticism and then to say, 'thank you'.

One recurring theme on feedback is the nature of the provider:

Feedback depends on who is giving it.

I need to trust the person I am getting feedback from.

I find it hard to accept criticism!

One interviewee recalled an observation from Professor Chris Witty that ran along the lines of 'do not put store on somebody's feedback who is not invested in you'. That seems like a key learning point and echoes the insight of Eleanor Roosevelt above!

Take a moment to analyse your own approach to reflection and how the process is informed by feedback. Where does your feedback come from? Let me suggest several options and decide which ones have the greatest resonance for you.

» Yourself

» Partner and close family

» Your mastermind group

» Close friends

» Work colleagues

» Random acquaintances and contacts.

I have three or four close friends and I am friendly with 30 or so people. I have loads of acquaintances, probably over 100.

The above list is in essence a reprise of the 'circles of influence' — Exercise 7 at the end of Chapter 3. The way the feedback is given will vary according to the nature of the relationship, the skill and sensitivity of the provider, and the context in which it is given. Most feedback occurs incidentally in informal situations, although some might be delivered through a formal structure, such as a school report or performance appraisal in the workplace.

If Shad Helmstetter[6] is right about us spending 90 per cent of our waking hours speaking to ourselves, then our own self-talk is a very significant strand in our feedback loop. We are most likely to receive a lot of feedback from the people we spend most time with. Our partner and close family both deliberately and accidentally provide information for us to weigh and act upon. The raison d'etre of our mastermind group is to supply support and challenge and this is another rich source of feedback. Close friends, work colleagues and random acquaintances and contacts may provide other feedback nuggets that are either positive or negative in nature.

The work of the five social scientists elaborated in Chapter 3 implicitly underscores the power of feedback and its influence on our development. We are social animals, and we are responsive to the actions and comments of others, particularly 'significant others'. Several interviewees highlighted the power of feedback from their parents that was either constructive or destructive. Encouragement features as a golden thread within the whole panoply of feedback varieties.

Feedback speaks into our world, and we decide how to respond to it. Our approach to reflecting on feedback may be consciously designed or simply our immediate response to random information. As I write this section, I am trying to deconstruct my own approach to reflection and to work out how it has changed over the years. Most reflection probably happens at the unconscious level as we are taking a shower or driving our car. It is background noise.

Travel gives my unconscious mind the time to do its work. I often have light bulb moments when I am travelling.

We may have more formal mechanisms to support focused reflection. My three favoured options in order of frequency are as follows.

» Talking things through with my wife

» Recording my reflections in my journal

» Engaging in formal coaching session with a skilled and insightful coach.

All three are ways of raising my thinking to the conscious level to examine it and modify it where appropriate – this is the heart of reflection. Some people are naturally more reflective than others, but I believe it is an approach to life than can be learned and developed. What do you think?

Angela Merkel never decides for 24 hours, and I think it is good to reflect. I'm told I'm a reflective person and I am also good at taking feedback. I try not to be defensive.

Peg 5: Mindset

The four pegs I have identified to support looking inwards – self-talk, story-telling, possibility thinking, feedback and reflection – are all component parts of our mindset. The mindset peg looms large in how we see ourselves. *The Free Dictionary*[22] defines mindset as:

A fixed mental attitude or disposition that predetermines a person's responses to and interpretation of situations

An inclination or habit.

This definition suggests that our mindset is fixed, and it predetermines our behaviour. Mindset provides the spectacles through which we view the world. Do you agree with his determinist assertion, or do you think it is possible to modify our mindset and thereby our behaviour? Mindset probably is an inclination or habit that is rarely challenged or interrogated. The tenor of this book lays bare my belief that we have agency and the possibility of change if we so desire. I espouse a positive mindset!

I must acknowledge here the feedback I have received from an unimpeachable source (my wife) that the positive mindset I champion can disappear in the face of setbacks, such as technological challenges or machinery breakdowns. I would argue, however, that despite these minor glitches I do maintain a positive mindset most of the time!

As I outlined in Chapter 1, mindset development is a dynamic process that reflects among other things, our history, our beliefs, our mood, and our view of the future. These elements are interactive and refuse to remain static but do provide a lens through which we interpret the events in and around us. Let us revisit Carol Dweck[23], and others who have built on her foundations, and start from the two basic mindsets:

A **fixed mindset** holds that your qualities are carved in stone. You have a certain level of intelligence, a certain personality, and a certain moral character. This is the hand you have been dealt.

A **growth mindset** is based on the belief that your basic qualities are things you can cultivate through your own efforts. Everyone can change and grow through experience.

The notion of fixed and growth mindsets provides a starting point to consider our prevailing approach to lifestyle development. Nevertheless, this duality may be too simplistic, and we manifest varying positions that shift along the fixed/growth continuum according to circumstances. Positive psychology holds that we can choose to change our mindset regardless of our previous experiences in life. The big question is *How do we do that?*

How would you describe your prevailing mindset? What is your default setting? I suggest you undertake some action research and note how you respond to critical incidents. Critical incident analysis is a way of analysing real incidents and building up a picture of your typical behaviours. Then work back to the thinking that underpins those behaviours and decide if you want to make changes in your habitual thinking patterns. Start with a very simple habit and design a programme of change.

As I age my mindset is changing. I discover new abilities.

Let me add a veneer of academic respectability to this approach by drawing on the work of three eminent researchers. Charles Duhigg in his book *The power of habit*[24] suggests that "To modify a habit you must decide to change it. You must consciously accept the hard work of identifying the cues and rewards that drive the habit's routines and find alternatives. You must know you have control and be self-conscious enough to use it." Duhigg recommends starting with keystone habits like healthy eating, regular exercise, or good timekeeping. Keystone habits offer what is known in the literature as small wins. The aggregation of small wins adds up to a big mindset win!

Barbara Fredrickson, quoted earlier in this chapter, emphasises the importance of nurturing a positive mindset. "Positivity reigns whenever positive emotions - like love, joy, gratitude, serenity, interest, and inspiration - touch and open your heart."[11] Her strategy is to seed more into our life – to increase our quantity of positivity over time. Our positivity ratio is the frequency of positivity over any chosen time span, divided by the frequency of negativity over that same time span. In mathematical terms, the ratio is captured by the simple expression P/N. Her prescription is to aim for a positivity ratio of at least 3:1.

This means that for every negative experience we endure we should endeavour to experience at least three positive experiences. This is the tipping point Fredrickson has identified in her research and this will predict whether we will flourish or languish. I prefer the sound of flourishing, but I realise that some people predicate their mindset upon being a victim and experiencing untold woes. This mindset is central to their persona, and the life story they tell, and they may not wish to relinquish it.

The notion of flourishing is one that has inspired a lot of research and one that has captured the collective imagination. Martin Seligman, the father of positive psychology, has authored a book simply entitled *Flourish*.[25] His thesis is that optimal functioning is tied to well-being and that optimism is a key precursor for success. He provides an excellent overview of the academic literature and furnishes the reader with a wide range of exercises to develop our flourish muscles. I have worked through his *Signature Strengths Test* and used it with a range of clients over the years.

The three academics I have quoted above all share a common focus on positivity, well-being, and happiness. They take slightly different routes to arrive at the same destination. Let me return to my starting point - the mindset peg. Mindset underpins and informs everything we do. Notwithstanding it is a slippery, multifaceted concept and one that a colleague once described as 'plaiting fog'. When in doubt go back to basics. Find a vocabulary to capture and describe your prevailing mindset. Pursue the action research approach I outlined above and record your findings in your journal.

My prevailing mindset is that of the eternal optimist, with a healthy dose of pragmatism. I am Socratic rather than Platonic. I search for the stars with my feet planted on the ground!

As a coach, I would recommend talking through your findings with a trusted other. Hearing yourself talk about your prevailing mindset and how you would like to develop it in the future provides you with the opportunity to find out what you are thinking. Skilled and empathetic questioning will add another dimension to this process.

Mindset development, like any change, requires both insight and commitment. Devising a plan is a sensible starting point.

Drawing together the strands

Looking inwards provides us with an opportunity to interrogate how we see ourselves. This could be seen as a selfish, self-indulgent exercise and yet I would still argue strongly that it is a healthy, and perhaps even altruistic undertaking. As an outcome of introspection, we are better prepared to interact successfully with others. Our self-concept underpins everything we do and is constructed from the beliefs we hold about ourselves. These beliefs are informed by our interactions with others and the feedback we receive over the course of our lives.

At the beginning of this chapter, I encouraged you to adopt a scientific approach to your excursion into introspection. I have suggested many and varied ways of looking inwards and have hung my approach on five chosen pegs in my mental changing room – self-talk, storytelling, possibility thinking, feedback and reflection, and mindset. Let me change the metaphor and ask you to consider these five pegs as a set of Russian dolls – a matryoshka. We may have different views about which is the largest and which is the smallest, but the salient point is that they all sit inside one another.

My matryoshka currently has **mindset** as the biggest doll, with the other four pegs stacking comfortably inside. Remembering that you are not restricted to my pegs, what does your matryoshka look like?

Living a conscious lifestyle involves increasing the impact of the elements of our lives that move us forward and decreasing the elements that hold us back. As you have studied this chapter you may have noticed the pairs of opposite words that crop up at various points. Let me highlight three pairs:

- » optimism and pessimism
- » positivity and negativity
- » opportunities and limitations.

The imperative of positive psychology is to increase the power of the first word in each pair, and to decrease the power of the second word. Thus, we become more optimistic, more positive, and see opportunities. We are less pessimistic, less negative, and circumnavigate limitations. This may be a little too simplistic and real life involves a much more nuanced approach. My view is that it is not either or, but rather a balance of… So, we will aim to be more optimistic and less pessimistic and so on.

I am my brand and that causes me to be more reflective.

You are the architect of your own life, and you have the power to choose the appropriate balance for you. Here are the two exercises flagged earlier to help with that process.

Exercise 8 My self-talk

This is an invitation to undertake a piece of action research over the coming month (30 days).

Listen intently to your own self-talk. Break this down into two parts:

The recurring scripts I run in my own head (private)

The recurring scripts I speak out and share with others (public)

Note these recurring scripts in your journal and take a moment to analyse them:

» What is the balance of positive and negative scripts?
» Which scripts would you like to change?
» Choose three scripts you would like to modify:
» Write the words
» See the picture
» Feel the emotions.

Write these three affirmations on a postcard or your phone using the following criteria:

» It is first person, singular – I
» It is present tense – this is what I do now
» It is active – I have agency
» It is positive – it highlights the benefits.

Repeat the affirmations at least a couple of times each day for the next month:

Catch yourself in the alpha state between waking and sleeping – first thing in the morning and last thing at night

Use spare moments to rehearse your new scripts

Review your progress at the end of the month

What will you repeat?

What do you plan to do differently?

Exercise 9 My Life Story

This exercise has been inspired by Bruce Feiler's work[15] and you can modify it to suit your own preferences.

Tell your own life story in 15 minutes. Resist the temptation to plan or write it out in advance. This is your own unscripted narrative.

Tell this story to a sympathetic listener and record what you are saying.

Play back the recording later and note anything you have found interesting about what you have said – for example:

» high points
» low points
» turning points.

Repeat the same exercise focusing on the sub-stories generated by the spokes on 'your Wheel of Life'.

Do you want to change parts of your story? Link back to Exercise 8 and repeat.

Set up a coaching session to reflect on how you intend to change your life story.

Bibliography

1. Aristotle – setquotes.com, 2. Carl Rogers – simplyppsychology.org, 3. Rosenthal, R & Jacobson, L (1968) Pygmalion in the Classroom, 4. David Taylor-Klaus – goodreads.com, 5. Louise Hay- thegoal.chaser.com, 6. Helmstetter, S (1986) What to Say When You Talk to Yourself, 7. Brownlee, A (2021) Relentless, 8. Denis Waitley – brainyquote.com, 9. National Storytelling Network – storynet.org, 10. Downing, E (2021) Coasting, 11. Fredrickson, B (2010) Positivity, 12. Betty Eadie – quotefancy.com, 13. Ursula Le Guin – terriwindling.com, 14. Thomas Merton – goodreads.com, 15. Feiler, B (2020) Life is in the Transitions, 16. Scott, A & Gratton, L (2020) The New Long Life, 17. Conley, C (2018) Wisdom at Work, 18. Tim Fargo - goodreads.com, 19. Cicero – thinkexist.com. 20. Eleanor Roosevelt – azquotes.com, 21. Merriam-Webster Dictionary – merriam-webster.com, 22. The Free Dictionary -thefreedictionary.com, 23. Dweck, C (2006) Mindset, 24. Duhigg, C (2012) The Power of Habit, 25. Seligman, M (2011) Flourish

A Focus on NOW

How to be the best you can be

The thesis of this book is that the life we are living NOW reflects the areas and themes we have explored in the previous four chapters.

The past: a reflection on your unique history (Chapter 1) provided the starting point for self-review. We are all unique and charting our history provides ample evidence of that fact. We see the world through the spectacles of our lived experience. The study of history is a worthwhile, and review of our personal history provides a rich source of self-discovery. Take time to reflect upon the key moments in your life and the significant people who have been an influence upon your development. The exercises at the end of Chapter 1 focused on your personal lifeline and your management of transitions. These exercises are designed to encourage you to reflect on your past life and to analyse how your unique history influences your behaviour NOW.

The future: the possibilities that lie ahead (Chapter 2), furnishes you with the opportunity to reflect upon your ideal future life. Your history has been charted and measured: your future life is of indeterminate length and quality. We do know that one out of one die and there will be an end point to our earthly life. We could die today or survive to receive a congratulations card from the King upon our hundredth birthday. The vision of the future you are nurturing gives shape and purpose to your lifestyle choices. Clarity of purpose simplifies life-planning and adds colour and texture to your existence. Your core values provide a starting point for constructing the life you desire. The wheel of life exercise provides a visual mechanism for reviewing where you feel you are today. Our future life is crammed with infinite possibilities if we can recognise them and take the appropriate action.

Looking outwards: understanding the wider world and our place in it (Chapter 3) explores the world that exists beyond ourselves. Several interviewees identified the desire to understand the world in much greater depth and the theorists summarised in this chapter provide a variety of contrasting starting points for this undertaking. From an early age, both consciously and unconsciously, we try to make sense of what is going on around us. People are social animals, and our first reference points are family and other care givers. Relationships permeate our growth and development and a sociogram provides one way of charting our significant relationships. The social circles exercise interrogates the nature of our relationships in a complementary way.

Looking inwards: understanding myself (Chapter 4) encourages both healthy introspection and robust self-analysis. Do I have to understand myself to understand the world, or is it the other way around? I suggest that looking outwards and inwards is not an either/or choice, rather each perspective informs the other. We seek to make sense of the world and our place in it. This process is made more complicated as the world is constantly changing and so are we. It is impossible to hold either or both still, as they are in a perpetual process of dynamic change. The five key strands elaborated in this chapter (*self-talk, storytelling, possibility thinking, feedback/reflection* and *mindset*) provide pegs to hang our thinking upon. The two exercises at the end of the chapter focus on the nature of our self-talk and our life story.

A focus on NOW — here we are at Chapter 5. This is where the four perspec-

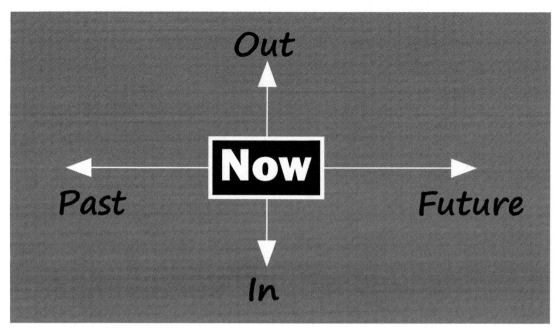

Figure 10 NOW seize the day

tives cohere, the nexus of the views from these four differing starting points. The location of your NOW on the dimensional cross will depend upon your age and stage. The older you are, the further the NOW will move across the horizontal axis. Similarly, it will move up or down the vertical axis depending on your interests and preference for looking outwards or inwards. Both axes are significant in locating your NOW. They each hold the other in balance. The purpose of this chapter is to draw together the recurring themes in the book and to help you make the most of your life NOW (Figure 10).

A popular prescription for living our best NOW has been attributed to the theologian Reinhold Niebuhr in what has become known as *The Prayer for Serenity*[1].

"God grant me the serenity to accept the things I cannot change,

The courage to change the things I can,

And the wisdom to know the difference."

A careful appraisal of those three elements – serene acceptance, courageous change, and discerning wisdom – provides the starting point for making the most of our NOW. As we reflect upon our current existence, what should we choose to accept and what should we endeavour to change? The discerning wisdom informs these choices. We have ranged over a variety of concepts, theories, and exercises as a preamble to making decisions about the life we desire. This is where the rubber hits the road, and we combine serenity, wisdom, and courage to chart our way forward.

A frequent topic with many of my coaching clients is achieving an appropriate work/life balance. The notion of **work/life balance** has come to the fore as well-being and mental health have moved up the collective entitlement agenda. In simple terms, **work** can be defined as the time you have sold to an employer – an organisation, employer, or even yourself. **Life** is a much more nuanced challenge to define – it could be seen as the time you are not being paid to work. This is a false dichotomy as our total existence is about life in all its fullness, including work. The key element in this discussion is **time** and the way we manage it. It has been said that effective time management is simply common sense, it is just not common practice!

The widely agreed components of effective time management are:

»   clear objectives and priorities – day, week, month, year(s)

- » daily plans and disciplines
- » a system for prioritising tasks
- » consistent diary management
- » ruthless with time, gracious with people.

A focus on NOW centres on living this moment. The past has gone, the future is yet to be. Live the present moment. There are a variety of ways of capturing this philosophy. The Roman poet Horace encouraged *carpe diem* - the imperative to seize the day. John Mark Comer[2] exhorts us to *inhabit the moment*. And the author that inspired me to think about the power of NOW, Eckhart Tolle. "Realise deeply that the present moment is all you have. Make now the primary focus of your life."[3] This is the focus of this chapter to reflect upon how to live this day to the full.

The notion of a journey is often employed as a metaphor for life. The starting point is birth, and the ultimate destination is death. The journey may be long, or it may be short – we do not know at the outset. When we examine the journey in more detail, we can see where we have been (*our history*) and Google Maps provides us with alternative ways forward (*our future*). We have choices about the route we take – motorways, main roads, or country lanes (*our route choices*). An analysis of our vehicle will guide the way forward (*our self-review*). We are all at different points on our journey of life and the challenge is to enjoy the scenery and to focus on the journey rather than the destination.

How do you conceptualise time and identify where you are on the journey of life? Gail Sheehy proposes a map of adult life which bears little scientific scrutiny but provides an interesting thought-starter. Zoom through her list and capture your responses. Here is her *new map of adult life*[4]:

- » try out 20s
- » turbulent 30s
- » flourishing 40s
- » flaming 50s
- » serene 60s
- » sage 70s
- » uninhibited 80s
- » nobility of the 90s
- » celebratory centenarians

Sheehy asserts that "The present never ages. Each moment is like a snowflake, unique, unspoiled, unrepeated, and can be appreciated in its surprisingness". I am excited by the possibility of making the most of each part of the journey. Although death is inevitable the way we live life is not! Each day provides new possibilities and opportunities to learn and grow.

> Do not settle for what you have got. I want to understand more about the world and my place in it.

> At 20 I wanted to change the world: at 56 I want to live one day at a time.

Using the metaphor of the journey, let us take time to review the vehicle you are driving. In the diagram below (Figure 11), the self is impacted by the mind, the body, and the spirit. The three circles (mind, body, and spirit) are all the same size in the diagram; this is rarely the case in real life.

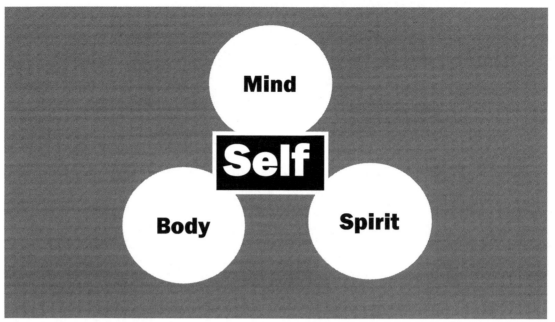

Figure 11 Self, Mind, Body, Spirit

The connections between mind, body and spirit shape who we are in this moment. When they are out of balance life becomes more difficult. Balance does not mean placing the same emphasis upon each of the three elements, but it does involve acknowledging the role of each element. We are more than just a living body that operates separately from mind and spirit. For example, a large proportion of illness emanates from the mind. Indeed pain is the relationship between the physical and the mental as Sarah Warren's excellent book *The Pain Relief Secret*[5] illustrates. She emphasises retraining your mind in order to heal your body and overcome chronic pain. A recurring theme in many of the interviews I undertook was the lack of emphasis on the spirit. Let us explore all three elements in more detail and pose the question *How balanced is my life now?*

Body

I was trained as a physical educator and began my working life as a teacher of physical education in a secondary school. In my mind at the time (1970s), my purpose was to help children and adults perform better in a range of sports by developing the relevant skills. I was particularly committed to soccer and gymnastics and coached both of these disciplines at a high level. Indeed, I became an accredited coach in six different sports and yet was never introduced to the mental side of *the game*. The emphasis was upon skill development, body conditioning and match awareness. It was all about the body: the mind and spirit were ignored.

The mental side of sport has come to the fore through the work of sports psychologists and psychiatrists like Dr Steve Peters. His book *The Chimp Paradox*[6] has changed the sporting landscape and the role of mental preparation has become widely acknowledged. I am developing a programme with a working title of *How to be the best you can be* for one of my grandchildren who is playing competitive basketball. My son, who is a keen golfer, is a disciple of 'Dr Bob'. One of Dr Rob Rotella's books is entitled *How Champions Think*[7] and that says it all! The role of the mind in the performance of the body pops up at every turn. How is it for you?

In Chapter 2, we explored the notion of health wealth. I recounted my own three-year research programme delving into the components of a healthy mind/body relationship, occasioned by back pain. One component of my recovery programme was to engage in sustained prayer, seeking guidance and restoration from God. This approach may not suit everybody, but I include it to underscore the links between body, mind and spirit in my personal philosophy. This book is not designed to evangelise or proselytise, it is intended to provide starting points for your own thinking. *What is your view on the links between body, mind, and spirit?*

Service intervals on modern cars have increased dramatically. I can remember having to have my car serviced at every 6000 miles and I was careful to have the service log completed meticulously as this impacted resale value! How is your body service log working? The National Health Service provides *Well Woman* and *Well Man* checks and a range of other screening procedures. These check points provide a bodily MOT – a state of play report on the body that may engender particular interventions. The advice of medical professionals is that prevention is better than cure and the admonition is to live a healthy lifestyle.

You will recall the Dr Victor Strecher mnemonic SPACE from Chapter 2 – *Sleep, Presence, Activity, Creativity, Eating*. These five components of robust health provide a helpful starting point in considering how to maintain a healthy body. They also impact our mental and spiritual health.

Sleep: this may feel like an odd starting point in the consideration of body maintenance and yet its role is often misunderstood or ignored. Indeed brain health is directly impacted by lack of revitalising sleep – the healthy brain needs time to repair and reboot. A closer look at the quality of our sleep can be be helpful and various watches and sleep aids are available to chart this. The purchase of a *Luminaire* clock will make a difference to falling asleep and waking up. The clock enables you to choose the colour of the light in your bedroom and the sounds that awaken you. I choose to wake up to a selection of birdsong. Take a closer look at the length and quality of your sleep. Sleep specialists suggest that sleep is far more important than diet or exercise and that sleep does not receive the priority it deserves!

Presence: in Chapter 2, I elaborated the *three Ms* in some detail - *Mindfulness, Meditation* and *Manifesting*. Presence involves a combination of all three and can be defined as paying attention to the NOW moment in a sustained way. Inhabiting the moment involves paying close attention to what you are feeling and thinking. One mindfulness exercise that I have found helpful is to examine a raisin for ten minutes. Concentrate on it to the exclusion of all else and allow different levels of seeing to emerge. Now use the same level of concentration to undertake your own body scan. You do not need an MRI scanner for this exercise, simply close your eyes and evaluate how your body feels as you shift your concentration and focus from the tips of your toes to the top of your head. Evaluate your current body state. Being able to be *fully present* in the moment is an enviable ability.

Activity: you can choose the exercise regime that suits your lifestyle, personality and physical state. A combination of cardio-vascular activities, weight training and stretching provides a sensible starting point. I enjoy walking and running, with the added bonus that it is very easy to record distances and times. I am less committed to strength training and the stretching is even more sporadic. You may do a physical job that demands particular movements and strength requirements in which case you may have a greater need to rest rather than exercise. For most of us, addressing the potential consequences of a sedentary lifestyle requires an exercise regime. January is the most popular month for joining a gym and engaging a personal trainer in an attempt to offset Christmas excesses. Review your physical, mental, and spiritual exercise regime.

My fitness regime includes yoga, running and swimming.

Creativity: when I first met my future wife, she was a dance student. Dance provides an excellent combination of physical, mental, and spiritual exercise. Indeed, most physical activities have the possibility to explore creativity. Can

I perform this movement in a different or better way? Can I modify the way I play this shot? Can I reconceptualise my approach to exercise? Keeping things fresh adds motivation to physical, mental, and spiritual activities. For most of us the challenge is to maintain motivation and to design a programme that works in the context of our unique circumstances. Time and money are significant considerations in embracing the multiplicity of possibilities creativity provides. Decide what works for you in your current circumstances.

Eating: we are very fortunate when we have the resources and choice to design our own diet. A high proportion of the world live below the poverty line and often go to bed hungry. The emergence of food banks in our first world western society underscores the challenges of being unable to feed yourself and your family. And yet many of us who have the resources to do so overeat and the prevalence of obesity bears testament to this fact. Eating is one of life's great pleasures. The old saying suggests that families that eat together, stay together. Shared meals can be a great social occasion for family and/or friends. We all have a diet: some may have more choice than others. Is your diet serving you or creating future problems for you?

My mother-in-law used to say, 'When you have your health, you have everything!'

I imagine that this woman was talking about physical health, although her aphorism could have also included mental and spiritual health.

Mind

Mind management is both a life-long challenge and a creative opportunity. In Chapter 1 I elaborated some of the formative influences on the way we think, notably:

» Parenting

» Role models and encouragement

» Formative experiences

» Value system

» Mindset.

Indeed, the previous four chapters have all invited you to reflect on how you think. Mental health wealth sits alongside the physical and exerts a powerful influence on the nature of our lives.

You don't notice good mental health until you are unwell, and then you really appreciate what you have lost.

The twin pillars of effective coaching are deemed to be self-awareness and responsibility. The same could be said of mental health. Can we become consciously aware of creating the conditions that will enable us to thrive and can we then take responsibility for maintaining robust mental health?

Evaluate the hand you have been dealt & make the most of it!

I am acutely aware of lacking the training and experience of a mental health professional and the insights I offer are offered as a layperson's thought starters. Mental ill health requires the care of specialists, and it is important to seek the appropriate expertise. The notion of a thought starter is that it stimulates your thinking. My intention is to invite you to reflect on how you manage your own mind. You are the expert in your own life – physical, mental, and spiritual.

Many years ago, I was attracted to a book entitled *The Silva Method* surprisingly written by a person called Jose Silva![8] The method is devoted to developing mind mastery. This is a seductive notion: a way to control your own thinking. I do not know how it is for you but sometimes my mind appears to have a life of its own and insists on building negative self-talk, impostor syndrome and catastrophic thinking into the same day. Some of Silva's chapter headings provide insights into his method: dynamic meditation, improving memory, speed learning, creative sleep, and improved health. 'Your words have power' is a particularly interesting chapter. What is your prescription for healthy mind management?

I am rarely ill. As children we were brought up by our parents to never be ill. We never had time off school!

Another element that bridges the mental, physical, spiritual divide is breathing. The importance of breathing cannot be overstated – when you stop breathing completely, you are dead! James Nestor, in his book *Breath*[9] describes breathing as the new science of a lost art. The book provides a fascinating scientific, cultural, spiritual, and evolutionary history of the way we breathe. The conclusion seems to be that most of us do it sub-optimally and would benefit from some breath work. *Breath* emphasises and enlightens us on how breathing and the mind are intertwined.

The other celebrity author who has caught the attention of an increasing number of people is Wim Hof *The Iceman*.[10] He describes his mission as shifting health care to self-care, and extols the virtues of conscious breathing, conscious mind control and exposure to cold. The television programme charting his work with a group of celebrities gave his ideas much wider currency in this country. *Wim Hof Method* accredited practitioners are now widely available, and a key element of their approach is breath work. I have found the breathing exercises extremely helpful and the cold showers much more of a challenge!

Both these writers believe that the capacity to enter our own brain starts with the breath. The breath is the door. Effective breathing enables us to meet the moment and let it teach us. In Hof's experimental groups the breathing practice and the exposure to cold was recorded as releasing the stress hormones adrenaline, cortisol, and norepinephrine on command. The notion of being able to open the brain's pharmacy on command to release self-produced opioids, dopamine and serotonin is transformational! I do feel enlivened by a cold shower (honestly)! The trick is to do the breathing exercise before turning the temperature down.

Let me take you back to the key question that underpins this section: 'How do you manage your mind?' You have consciously and unconsciously developed your mind management habits over the course of your life, and I am inviting you to reflect on the strategies that serve and those that do not. Let's revisit some of the key concepts on a whistle-stop tour of mind management.

Age and stage theories provide insights into your physical and mental development (Chapter 3).

Your unique history influences the nature of your thinking (Chapter 1) and the way you perceive the world.

Education in the widest sense provides a variety of lenses through which to understand the world and your place in it (Chapter 1).

The roots and branches of your life provide a structure that shapes your thinking (Chapter 2) and opens future possibilities.

The five pegs that support your journey inwards (Chapter 4) help you to interrogate and understand your own thinking processes.

For me mental health is feeling happy in my own skin and keeping life simple. I care less about what other people think and concentrate on what I think!

The mind has been likened to an unbroken horse, it rears and bucks and needs careful handling. It takes time, perhaps a lifetime to learn how to manage it. You are the expert in your own life, and you can choose how you wish to think!

My mental fitness regime involves psychotherapy, coaching and meditation.

Spirit

Question 9 in my interview schedule generated some interesting responses: 'How do you manage your health (physical, mental and spiritual)?' All my interviewees answered the physical part of the question with great gusto and most of them were very lucid in connection with the mental. The spiritual section generated very different responses and appeared to induce discomfort and uncertainty.

I am not spiritual, I feed my soul through nature and the beach.

I am ethical and moral, rather than spiritual.

As a non-directive interviewer, I endeavoured to ask follow-up questions to coax an answer on how the person manages spiritual health. It seemed that many of my respondents interpreted the question as being about whether they follow a particular faith. Three interviewees indicated that the spiritual side of their life was something they had not yet got round to.

Is faith the next phase?

My last book was entitled *Living a Christian Lifestyle* and was clearly written from a particular faith standpoint. The sub-title captured my motivation for writing the book: *30 bite-sized steps to move closer to God*. I am a Christian and my faith informs everything I think and do. God is at the centre of my life. At a basic level my spiritual disciplines include prayer, bible-study, and fellowship (spending time with other Christians). My spirituality manifests itself in a mainline faith that guides my life. Friends and acquaintances follow other faiths or no faith at all.

Some theologians suggest that every person is born with a need to find God – a God-shaped hole in their lives that needs filling. A large proportion of the world's population are signed up to a particular faith and its attendant philosophy. A proportion pursue a life that is militantly antagonistic to any kind of faith and reject 'the opium of the people'. A further proportion, either by design or default, have not spent any time or energy investigating their own spiritual needs. Those positions were all represented in the answers to Question 9.

This book is about living a conscious lifestyle and I am inviting you to review your spirituality in its widest form, whether that is a mainline religion or an appreciation of nature and the beach. Investigation involves searching that leads to recognising and appreciating.

I need reflection days.

I want to sit back and think more.

One of the responses I received at the end of most of the interviews indicated that the questions had caused people to reflect at a deeper level than usual. One respondent asked if his partner could sit in on the interview to understand what he was thinking. This request caused me to ruminate on how deeply people understand one another.

I see spirituality as connecting with others.

Collective worship is about awe and wonder and people acting in union. I never cease to be amazed at how 40 000 football fans at the *Stadium of Light* (Sunderland AFC's ground) can sing in unison without any obvious direction. Is this a spiritual experience in the widest sense? Undoubtedly when we win it is an experience that lifts the spirits! School assemblies, worship services, baptisms, weddings, and funerals are all opportunities to manifest shared spirituality. Connecting with others offers much more than that and looking inwards at our own spirituality provides a rich seam for further exploration.

"Someday your life will be over, no matter how much attention you give to your health. Will you look back with regret because you nourished your body but starved your soul?"[11] Contemplation, prayer, and meditation are all vehicles into our inner space. These mental disciplines detach us neurologically from our habitual ways of thinking and seeing. The move from left-brain hurry to right-brain stillness enables us to interrogate our inner world.

The power of NOW, this moment, lies in seeing with new eyes what has become habitual and taken for granted. Richard Rohr in his book *Just This*[12] frames it elegantly in the following suggestion:

> **"To let the moment teach us, we must allow ourselves to be at least slightly stunned by it until it draws us inward and upward, toward a subtle experience of wonder. We normally need a single moment of gratuitous awe to get us started – and such moments are the only solid foundation for the entire religious instinct and journey."**

The spiritual journey is characterised by allowing ourselves to be captured by the goodness, truth, or beauty of something beyond and outside us. The ego resists awe and our will resists surrender and yet both are significant in spiritual awareness. Rohr contends that the NOW is the way to the always and the material is the way to the spiritual. How would you evaluate your spiritual health?

I am concentrating on just 'being'.

The interrelatedness of the physical, mental, and spiritual makes self-review complicated. Once again, it is difficult to hold one or two of the elements still to evaluate the impact of the other. Right NOW, we are inhabiting our physical body, exercising our logical mind, and living a spiritual experience that we will never have again. The notion of balance is a seductive one: placing appropriate emphasis upon the physical, mental, and spiritual simultaneously. My conclusion is that we probably put the physical at the top of our pecking order, mental second and the spiritual can come in a distant third. How is it for you?

I don't want any more materially and yet I feel I have a spiritual deficit.

Two other recurring themes emerged from the interviews: the significance of time and money, and the importance of particular people.

Time and money

This chapter is devoted to considering the power of NOW and the choices we make in inhabiting the moment. These choices are influenced by the amount of discretionary time and financial resources we have at our disposal.

I am lucky to have enough money to do what I please. I live a comfortable life. I don't do anything I don't want to do.

This interviewee was not bragging about her wealth and possessions, rather she was highlighting that financial plenty provides a wider range of possibilities and choices. As we have rehearsed earlier, material wealth allows people to purchase goods and services and liberates more time to do the things you choose to do. Every chosen activity has an *opportunity cost* (if I did not to do that, I could be doing something else). My interviewees all live in a first world country and enjoy varying levels of material wellbeing, as do my potential readers. For people struggling below the poverty line the lack of discretionary time and financial resources constrains their level of choice.

How much is enough? is a challenging book written by the father and son team of Robert and Edward Skidelsky[13]. Let me pose the question to you directly: how much money do you require to live the good life? Fumio Sasaki[14] argues for minimalist living as a method for finding happiness and meaning. There is not necessarily a correlation between your bank balance and your level of happiness, but it would be naïve to suggest that your level of wealth does not impact your life choices. Writing this section feels uncomfortable: *how does it feel reading it?*

> *It is a great joy to be able to do what you please.*

This interviewee was enjoying the early fruits of a comfortable retirement, released from the constraints of the world of paid work. To a greater or lesser extent, we all have the facility to create our own inner world, particularly the mental and spiritual domains, regardless of our material wealth. However, as Victor Frankl discovered in the prison camp, people respond very differently to the same external circumstances.

Levels of wealth may vary, but for all of us time is a finite, and scarce resource.

> *I am seeking clarity on how to use time wisely.*

> *I want to develop myself and spend more time with my family.*

This last statement leads into another theme emerging from the interviews: the importance of particular people.

Significant people

> *My Dad's death reinforced the importance of grasping every opportunity and living every day as if it is your last.*

This is a *carpe diem* approach to life, that underscores the importance of both significant people and scarcity of time. Several interviewees emphasised the impact of serious illness in helping to establish the importance of relationships and time management choices. Their illness was a wake-up call.

> *Cancer pushed me forward!*

The notion of finding the opportunity in even the direst situations is addressed later in this chapter, under the title of 'obstinacity'. Relationship breakdown, illness, and even bereavement can present unexpected opportunities.

> *Sometimes life throws negativity in your path and it cracks you open. You become vulnerable and crushed, and you decide to let others in.*

We are designed to be in relationship with others. Close relationships involve the interplay of giving and receiving. The *Social Circles Exercise* in Chapter Three was designed to chart your significant people. My interviewees repeatedly emphasised the importance of close family and friends. Deborah James DBE and 'bowel babe' put it brilliantly before her untimely death when she asserted "My priorities changed completely after cancer. The desire to live well and forge even more meaningful relationships with people I love was what mattered most".[15]

Love manifests itself in many forms:

   » **Agape:** altruistic, selfless, unconditional love

- » **Eros:** romantic, passionate, physical love
- » **Philia:** love for friends
- » **Philautic:** self-love
- » **Storge:** parent-child love.

An in-depth study of the various forms of love and the love languages[1] that sustain them is beyond the scope of this book. However, I would like to briefly highlight the importance of *agape* and *philautic* love.

Heidi Baker, who leads *Iris Ministries* serving the children on the rubbish dumps of Mozambique, captured the essence of agape when she was asked how she could possibly meet the needs of the abandoned children in the city. Her answer was powerful in its simplicity "I will love the one in front of me". This is an excellent prescription for changing the world for the better, one person at a time. *Agape love* could be seen as a turbo-charged version of encouragement!

Philautic love is love of the self. In modern societies this is often associated with being narcissistic, selfish, and self-centred. This was not the original meaning attributed to philautic love: originally it represented the notion of being able to give and receive love from others. Indeed, it could be argued that self-love and self-care are altruistic as they build greater capacity to serve others. In this way agape and philautic love are closely related. We cannot give to others what we do not have.

Spend more time with the people you love and build meaningful relationships. Cut adrift casual relationships.

The second sentence in the above quote at first sight appears callous and yet on closer inspection emphasises the importance of devoting quality time to the people you love. Prioritising the allocation of your time and energy to 'loved ones' seems eminently sensible. This realisation created the impetus for me to establish our Family Learning Community. Two of my greatest passions in one place: family and learning. A monthly on-line session where the adults in the family meet for a shared learning experience.

How is your love life? This is not intended to be an intrusive question, rather I am inviting you to think about love in the widest sense. "Ultimately the quality of our relationships will determine the quality of our lives."[17]

The self-efficacy cube:
How to be the best you can be

In this final section of the book, I would like to provide a distillation of the ground we have covered. My challenge to you is to create your own unique synthesis that will enable you to live a conscious lifestyle. I have identified nine recurring themes that have appeared and reappeared throughout the book. These golden themes are summarised in *The Self-efficacy Cube* below. I invite you to use this cube to scaffold your thinking.

"The past is behind you, learn from it. The future is ahead of you, prepare for it. The present is here, live it."[18]

These nine golden themes form the basis of my *How to be the best you can be* programme. Self-efficacy is at the centre of the cube and you can decide the order in which you choose to address the other themes. It is difficult to disentangle the themes as they criss-cross and overlap. Life is like that, and the diagram could be viewed as your life's *Rubik's Cube* that you can manipulate to suit your current circumstances. Each theme ends with an exercise/challenge to deepen your thinking.

Health Wealth

The greatest wealth

Self-care

Feedback & Reflection

Input from others

Considerationof feedback & reflection

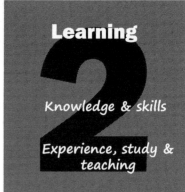

Learning

Knowledge & skills

Experience, study & teaching

Encouragement

Support

Confidence

Hope

Self-efficacy

To be the best you can be

The best version of myself

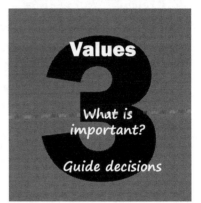

Values

What is important?

Guide decisions

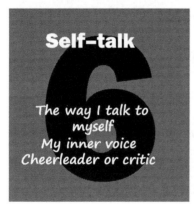

Self-talk

The way I talk to myself
My inner voice
Cheerleader or critic

Possibility Thinking

5a

Possibilities v. limitations

Mindset

5b

Open v. closed
Positive v. negative

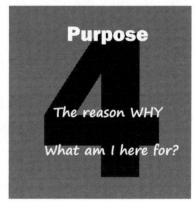

Purpose

The reason WHY

What am I here for?

Self-efficacy: you are the expert in your own life

"Throughout my athletics career, the overall goal was always to be a better athlete than I was now – whether next week, next month, or next year. The improvement was the goal. The medal was simply the ultimate reward for achieving that goal."[23]

The two-time Olympic gold medal winner Sebastian Coe epitomises the desire to be the best you can be. Initially coached by his father, he ultimately took responsibility for his own performance – he became the expert in his own life. This mindset took him to the pinnacle of world athletics and personal fulfilment. We may not be an Olympic athlete, but we can still relentlessly pursue expertise in our chosen field.

Our NOW is located on the horizontal axis between the past and the future. The psychological theories elaborated in Chapter 3 provide a variety of lenses to magnify how we have become who we are today. These theories may or may not be useful, but what is certain is that we have lived a life thus far that can be analysed as an ongoing experiment. The decision about where to go next and where to grow next is ours! This is at the heart of living a conscious lifestyle. No social theorist knows the intimate details of our past or the shape of our future aspirations. We have an infinite number of choices, and we have the power to make them for ourselves.

"In our offices and our classrooms, we have way too much compliance and way too little engagement."[24] Despite espousing otherwise, workplaces and schools value conformity and compliance. If we cannot be fully engaged in our own lives and the lives of the people we love, where can we get excited?

Self-actualisation is a motivating force that merits close attention and personal investment. My understanding of self-actualisation is that it sits at the top of Maslow's hierarchy of needs. It is the overwhelming desire to maximise our abilities and opportunities – to be the best we can be. The nature of self-actualisation will vary from person to person as each one is the expert in their own unique life.

How are you doing in realising your **full potential**? The boundaries of *full potential* are hard to establish. Young children discover boundaries by pushing their caregivers, (parents, carers, or teachers) till they are told to stop what they are doing. As adults, most of our boundaries are illusory and self-imposed. We are influenced by others – by societal norms and particularly by the nature of our mastermind group. This is an argument for choosing your mastermind group carefully! Exercises 6 and 7 encouraged you to review your social contacts: the sociogram and social circles chart your relationships with the people close to you. These people are undoubtedly influential, and I say again, you are the expert in your own life!

Exercise 10 Self-efficacy

When you acquire a new car or purchase a new gadget you take time to figure out how to maximise their performance. Being the best you can be requires you to figure out what works for you and what does not. Approach the questions below in a spirit of discovery and record your immediate answers, then take some time to reflect upon what you have written.

What learning behaviours worked for me as a child?

How have I modified my approach to learning as an adult?

How does my mastermind group influence me?

Where do I want to grow in the next chapter of my life?

What experiences and activities excite and motivate me?

How can I be the best I can be?

Learning: continue to be a learner

"Anyone who stops learning is old, whether at twenty or eighty. Anyone who keeps learning stays young."[19] Eternal youth is probably not my primary motivation to be a lifelong learner, but it is a useful bonus. Lifelong learning starts in the womb and ends on the deathbed. The possibilities are infinite. Early learning starts in the home, and progresses through primary, secondary, tertiary and/or vocational education. Lifelong learning is not restricted to formal educational experiences but embraces the wider education derived from the university of life. Self-initiated education is possible at any age but typically flourishes at the end of, or in spaces between, formal programmes.

The significance of learning has reappeared at various points in this book. Your unique history reviewed in Chapter 1, included your parenting, your school experiences and the influence of significant teachers and role models. These experiences have undoubtedly shaped your view of education. Your future learning was explored in some detail in Chapter 2. The world is your oyster: you can learn whatever you choose to learn. This is an exciting prospect. Chapter 3 emphasised further the notion that you are the expert in your own life, and you can select the educational experiences that suit your chosen life course.

Whether we are pursuing personal passions or chasing qualifications, lifelong learning can help us achieve personal fulfilment and satisfaction. We have more measuring points in our formal education system than any other country in the world and I believe this approach can encourage us to see education as a series of hurdles to be jumped. This reductionist approach can foster a narrow concept of education. Throw off the shackles of this restricted view and embrace the breadth of possibilities education provides. Keep learning.

One famous person is alleged to ask his family and friends 'What have you learned since we last met?' This is a great question. It could be expanded to enquire what you have learned since we met, and what are you planning to learn next? As humans, we have an innate drive to explore, learn, and grow. I believe our quality of life is immeasurably enhanced by lifelong learning. So, what are you motivated to learn next? Let me frame this question in more depth in the following exercise.

Exercise 11 Learning

Chart your lifelong learning journey, both the formal and informal parts.
What does it look like so far?
What feelings does this chart generate?
Next consider what you would like to learn next.
What inspires and excites you?
What new learning would you like to explore?
Acknowledge the practical implications of your educational plans.
How much time have you got to invest?
How much money are you prepared to invest?

Values: make them visible

Your core values define who you are. "Values are like fingerprints. Nobody's is the same, but you leave them all over everything you do."[20] Take time to interrogate your own value system as this is the launch pad of your future success. Your core values are the deeply held beliefs about yourself and the world that guide your behavioural choices. Clarity about your value system simplifies decisions about when to say *Yes*, and when to say *No*.

"Keep your thoughts positive because your thoughts become your words. Keep your words positive because your words become your behaviour. Keep your behaviour positive because your behaviour becomes your habits. Keep your habits positive because your habits become your values. Keep your values positive because your values become your destiny."[21]

Mahatma Gandhi's quotation suggests the chain of life has several interlocking links: *thoughts – words – behaviour – habits - VALUES – destiny*. Values have a starring role in this chain that is infused with positivity. I have devoted time to reflecting on the values that drive me. At the time of writing, my life is driven by the values of integrity, wisdom, serenity, and authenticity. These are displayed in a prominent position in my study and underpin my vision and mission statements. What are the core values that drive you?

Analysing how you developed your core values is an interesting research project. In Chapter 1 we ranged over the influence of our parenting, role models and the formative experiences that shaped our emerging value system. Education and the world of work provide proving grounds for the longevity of these values. Those of us who become parents or co-workers ourselves have additional opportunities to share our values with others. Faith provides yet another overlay on the refinement of our value system.

In Chapter 2, we considered values as one of the 'roots' that anchors my tree of life. Roots are designed to go deep and provide stability. What you see above the ground mirrors the growth that is going on below the ground. Exercise 4 was designed to help you uncover your core values and life purpose. These two things are inextricably linked and inform the ability to live a truly conscious lifestyle.

Exercise 12 Values

Revisit Exercise 4 and focus on the four or five core values you identified.

What are they?

How do you make them visible?

Focus on one value at a time – meditate, reflect, note the outcome.

What do you notice?

How does this value inform your behavioural choices?

The future

Will these values serve you for the rest of your life?

What do you want 'more of' and what do you want 'less of'?

Purpose: live life on purpose

"There are two great days in a person's life – the day we are born and the day we discover why."[22] The date of our birth is recorded for posterity on our birth certificate, the day we discover why we are born is much harder to determine. Some children know what they want to do early in life, while some adults only discover their calling in their end days. Knowing your life purpose is a significant step towards living a truly conscious lifestyle. Discovering our life purpose provides us with a vision of the future we will endeavour to make a reality. Clarity of purpose facilitates decision making and life choices.

In Chapter 2, I identified purpose as another of the roots that anchor our tree of life. Roots are important when the wind blows, and storms threaten to engulf us. We considered the health and longevity benefits that accrue from having clarity of purpose. Viktor Frankl observed at first hand the endurance of those prison camp inmates who had a reason to survive - a *why* to carry on living in the most horrendous of circumstances. The purpose-driven inmates outlived their physically stronger contemporaries! We should not underestimate the power of the role purpose plays in our existence.

At times life can seem very complicated: it does not have to be! Discovering your purpose is a simplifying process that clarifies and establishes what you are living for.

I value expensive cars, exotic holidays and playing golf.

This quotation is an interviewee's summary of a much more complicated answer. I have included it to illustrate what human performance researchers have known for years: complex goals are easier to achieve if they are broken down into simpler ones. Financial goals, like the above, are much easier to measure than quality of life goals, although the two are often inextricably linked.

How clear is your purpose? I have written my purpose statement and it is displayed in a prominent place in my study to remind me of why I am committed to what I do. There are two slightly different versions.

The public version: to help people be the best they can be – the best version of themselves.

The private version: to love and serve my God and to love and serve my family.

What is yours?

Where I am now reflects both growth and purpose.

Purpose highlights what is important to us and what is not. Decisions about the allocation of time and energy, in my view, should be driven by the question *Is this manifesting my purpose?*

The two themes we have already discussed (learning and values) are closely linked to purpose. Values shape the environment within which purpose can flourish. Future learning choices are influenced by what we are seeking to achieve.

I love work, it gives me energy for the other parts of my life.

Exercise 13 Purpose

I suggest that once again you revisit Exercise 5 and review your answers in the light of this section on purpose. I have identified seven key points below – evaluate the impact of each one in relation to purpose in your life.

Clarity of purpose supports health and well-being and protects against disease and death.

Purpose is a high-level goal that motivates action.

The values that constitute purpose matter.

Purpose in life reduces defensiveness to change.

Your purpose in life might be revealed by God (Holy Purpose) but it might not.

Purposeful living is a dynamic process that requires energy and will power.

Purposeful living is not just a higher order aspiration for the well-educated. It is for everyone!

Possibility Thinking: recognising opportunities when you see them

(Theme 5 is subdivided into two interlocking sections – possibility thinking and mindset.) Possibility thinking is the bedrock of a growth mindset. At a fundamental level, it is the willingness to search for opportunities rather than blockages. The future beckons with endless possibilities if only we can recognise them when they appear. In Chapter 2 we explored the branch of our future tree that has possibilities carved into its bark. The growth potential of this branch can be seen as limitless, or limited, or somewhere in between – the choice is yours. When in doubt, take a risk and go for it!

One of my growth experiences was to attend the *Coverdale Team Coaching Programme*. Three separate residential weeks emphasised the importance of seeing the opportunities embedded in every situation. Indeed, the *Coverdale Organisation* had invented its own word for always focussing on the positive. The word is *obstinacity* and it is impossible to find it in any dictionary. For me, the word summarises the imperative to seek the positive elements of even the direst of situations. For example, a famous artist only began to paint after she had broken her leg and was confined to the house.

As you look back through your life can you identify examples of obstinacity, where an opportunity has emerged from a difficult situation? A recent example for me was provided by the pandemic that forced me to change the way I conduct my business. I could not see people in person, so my coaching was moved on-line. This saved an enormous amount of travel time and caused us to dispense with one of our two cars. Savings in both time and money.

Seligman's research[25] alluded to in Chapter 2 highlighted the importance of aptitude, motivation, and the magic ingredient – optimism. Aptitude and expertise help us to recognise the inherent possibilities in any situation. Motivation provides us with the desire to maximise the possibilities in that situation. And optimism gives us the mindset to believe that success is possible. New Year's Resolutions are usually short-lived and doomed to failure because they lack the substance and planning to make them a reality. This need not be so when recognising that the opportunity is simply the first link in the chain of turning a possibility into a living reality.

We have far more choices than we realise, and the challenge is to open our eyes wide enough to see them. Our *reticular activation system* (RAS), that made an appearance in Chapter 2, is designed to spot opportunities. The RAS is an automatic goal seeking mechanism located in the brain that needs to be programmed to scan for the opportunities you crave. We can approach the future with boundless optimism or disillusioned pessimism. Both approaches will programme the RAS to identify possibilities that support that particular view of the world. Optimism increases possibilities, pessimism closes them down – possibility thinking versus impossibility thinking. Once again, the choice is yours.

Mindset: growth and optimism

"Certainty is a cruel mindset. It hardens our minds against possibility."[26] Possibility thinking and mindset are inextricably linked. We can choose our mindset – fixed/pessimistic thinking or growth/optimistic thinking. I suspect it would be almost impossible to live 24 hours per day in growth/optimistic mode, but my aspiration is to increase the percentage. Apart from anything else, optimists feel better and are more fun to be with. I am more optimistic when I spend time with optimists and despite my best intentions pessimists can drag me closer to

their level of despondency. I have choice about how I decide to manage my own thinking and who to spend time with.

Mindset is not fixed and could be seen as being in a constant state of flux. Nevertheless, we all develop idiosyncratic ways of seeing the world and it requires conscious effort to evaluate what ways of thinking and frames of mind are shaping our predominant mindset. In Chapter 2, we explored mindset as one of the roots of your tree of the future. Chapter 4 highlighted mindset as one of the pegs to support looking inwards. Our personal history underpins our mindset development – upbringing, education, peer groups and culture are some of the contributors to this process.

In short, our mindset shapes how we perceive the world and our place in it. It is like a pair of spectacles we never take off. The prescription may change over time, and we may choose different frames, but mostly we just take these spectacles that engender specific ways of seeing for granted. The spectacles influence how we think, feel, and behave. Most of this happens at the unconscious level. I am inviting you to focus on your mindset and lift it up to the conscious level. Do you want to make changes? What is serving you and what is not serving you?

> *My positive outlook is very important. I don't worry about what I cannot change.*
>
> *I accept what I cannot do anything about.*

These two interviewees are clearly proponents of the *Prayer for Serenity* and have made a conscious choice to focus on what can be changed. It is noteworthy that almost all my interviewees were clearer on what they want 'more of' and less clear on what they want 'less of' (Question 10). Is it easier to embrace positive change than to jettison life-long habits? New Year's Resolutions often seem doomed to failure as the conscious mind grabs the steering wheel of life and the unconscious mind says wait and see and takes us back to our habitual ways of doing things.

Andrew Castle was interviewed for the *Lessons from a life in sport* in the Sunday Times on July 24th, 2022, and he revealed one of his key learning points concerning mindset. "I learnt most from not saying no. Say yes, take a risk, even if it makes your nervous and uncomfortable. If you try and fail, that's fine, because sometimes you'll try and succeed."[27] This approach combines positive mindset and possibility thinking!

Exercise 14 Possibility thinking

Over the next few days identify two or three situations to interrogate in some detail. Describe each situation in a neutral, detached way – the bare bones of what is going on.

Now look at the bare bones through a possibility thinking lens (obstinacity) – what are the positive opportunities that the situation presents?

Reverse the telescope and imagine all the negative outcomes that could accrue from the same situation.

What do you notice when you compare the positive and negative possibilities? Choose one focus to concentrate your RAS upon. Look for possibilities in both obvious and unexpected places.

Exercise 15 Mindset

Invest time in evaluating your prevailing mindset. Here are several activities to scaffold your thinking.

Challenge your prevailing mindset by seeking out people who think differently to you. Adam Grant[8] calls this 'escaping the echo chamber' of groupthink where everybody thinks the same. Identify two or three people who will challenge your view of the world, engage them in debate, and really listen to what they have to say.

Embrace the possibility of being wrong. This is particularly challenging in close relationships when we have a strong desire to prove we are right all the time! (My wife frequently supplies me with this developmental feedback!) Develop a mindset that sees mistakes as disguised learning opportunities. In the coming week, note two or three examples of where being wrong led to new learning.

Adopt a growth mindset more often. It is not enough to know about a growth mindset, the important part is to practise it! Pursue a similar approach to the two activities already outlined. In the coming week recognise instances of where you are employing a fixed mindset in your thinking and behaviours and consciously seek to change them. You may wish to enlist the support of a person you trust, family member or friend, or avail yourself of the services of a coach.

Note the outcomes of these activities in your learning journal. Remember we are all a work in progress and always maintain a growth/optimistic mindset!

Self-talk: what you say when you talk to yourself

Self-talk is one of the most powerful weapons in our armoury. What we say to ourselves each day has a profound effect upon self-image and behaviour. As I emphasised in Chapter 4, I believe self-talk can be changed with conscious practice. The inner voice that commentates on what you are thinking and doing can either be a force for good or a destructive critic. The challenge is to increase the former and reduce the latter. In this way, positive self-talk builds us up, while negative self-talk knocks us down. The key is to listen to what we say to ourselves.

Self-talk shapes our self-image, which in turn influences our behaviour. Habitual self-talk scripts are grooved early in life. These scripts started out as conscious thoughts that have become beliefs and biases. These are the spectacles through which we see and interpret the world. Take time to review your self-talk scripts and decide which ones are serving you and which ones are not. Strengthen the ones that are serving you and jettison the ones that are not.

The language we use to frame our inner dialogue is significant. It is instructive to listen carefully to the language of family, friends, and work colleagues to illustrate this process. Positive language generally begets positive outcomes and negative language is equally effective in generating undesirable results. Stephanie Davies, the author of *Laughology*[29], has constructed a model that captures the importance of the language we choose – she has entitled it *FLIP*. *F* is for focus, *L* is for language, *I* is for imagination, and *P* is for pattern breaking. The language section is particularly significant: it is not only about what we say, but how we say it.

Neuroplasticity is the physical process of the brain rewiring itself and the nature of the language we choose is influential in this process. Sports psychology places a heavy emphasis on the importance of positive self-talk to bring our best game at the crucial moment. As Alistair Brownlee emphasised in *Relentless*[30], self-talk is a significant part in developing a winning mindset. We may not be an Olympic champion, but we still want to be the best we can be. The great news is that we can change the balance of our self-talk by increasing the percentage that is positive and reducing the percentage that is negative. To always be one hundred percent positive may be an impossible challenge, but with practice we can certainly shift the balance.

The benefits of positive self-talk are innumerable. Research shows that physical and mental health are improved, self-esteem increases, and anxiety and stress are reduced. It costs nothing and has the potential to generate great results. The inner critic and impostor syndrome will seek to subvert your progress, turn the volume down on the negative and amplify the positive. Revisit Exercise 8 in the last chapter: review the progress you made over the thirty days and map your way ahead.

Exercise 16 Self-talk revisited

What did you notice about your private and public scripts?

What is the balance of positive and negative scripts, and have you been able to shift that balance?

Focus on the scripts you sought to modify using the strategy of write the words, see the picture, feel the emotions – how much progress have you made?

Review the affirmations you wrote and the structure for constructing them (first person, present tense, active, and positive) – has this approach become second nature?

Add an extra layer of focus on the language you are using when you talk to yourself – drown out the inner critic and beef up the positivity.

Encouragement: the perfume of success

"You don't need to be better than anyone else, you just need to be better than you used to be."[31] Encouragement is a vital component of self-talk. Give yourself the benefit of the doubt and focus on your successes. Note your large and small successes as you progress through each day.

This strand of encouragement is entirely within our own control and represents a mindset choice. The process is enhanced further by spending time with people who are 'encouragers': your mastermind group and others who can supply encouragement in various ways. It is sensible to seek out people who will provide the type of encouragement you thrive on.

To encourage literally means to give courage, confidence, and hope to yourself or to another. I have heard encouragement likened to spraying perfume on people: when you splash it on others you almost always get some on yourself! Some of the saddest responses from my interviewees relate to not being encouraged, particularly as children. Indeed, some were actively discouraged and bore the scars for many years.

In Chapter 1, I asked you to identify your significant role models, with a particular focus on encouragement. Take a moment now to visualise those people and reflect on how they encouraged you. Fast forward to NOW and ask yourself who are the people who encourage you in this phase of your life. What do they do and say that you find encouraging? How does being encouraged make you feel?

Crudely we could divide people into three groups – encouragers, neutrals, discouragers. Encouragers are usually warm and generous, they take an interest in you, and give you a warm glow. The neutrals are neither warm nor cold, they appear emotionless and matter of fact and do not generate any strong feelings either way. The discouragers may or may not set out to rain on your parade — they often say *That is just how I am*. They are capable of deliberately or accidentally inflicting collateral emotional damage on the people around them. My conclusion is a very simple one: spend as much time as possible with the people who will encourage you and the minimum amount of time with discouragers.

Encouraging others is a gift to society. It is a mindset. It displays emotional generosity.

> *I try to see the good in everyone! We create the weather for the people around us – this is particularly important with children.*

It is challenging to be relentlessly encouraging when you don't get anything back. *The Bible* teaches that it is more blessed to give rather than to receive, and yet no matter how sophisticated or generous we are, we still need encouragement. For this reason, I believe it is important to nurture relationships with accomplished encouragers. As Michelle Obama suggests "We need to do a better job of putting ourselves higher on our to do lists."[32] Let me invite you to do that right now.

Exercise 17 An encouragement audit

Identify the encouragers, neutrals, and discouragers in your current life.

Name the role models who encouraged you in your childhood and early adult life – how did they make you feel?

Identify your top three encouragers NOW.

How accomplished are you at encouraging others?

Name the people you have encouraged in the last week.

Who will you seek to encourage in the next week?

What concrete action grows out of this audit?

Specify who, what, and when.

Health Wealth

"If you don't make time for wellness, you may be forced to make time for illness. Not all health problems are caused by our lifestyle, but some are."[33] These cautionary words from Professor Paul McGee capture the essence of this theme. Good health is often taken for granted until it disappears. You cannot guarantee that you will live to a hundred and never be ill! The possibility of minor or serious illness is part of life, but we can increase the likelihood of staying fit by adopting a healthy lifestyle. As one interviewee put it:

> *Look at the hand you have been dealt & make the most of it!*

Several other interviewees highlighted incidences of serious illness and the impact it had had on their mindset (See Chapter 1). They realised they were not

immortal and that it is important to 'seize the day'. In this way, a positive 'carpe diem' philosophy grew out of very challenging and frightening circumstances. Physical health and mental health are bidirectional – one impacts the other. We feel better mentally when we are physically fit. Likewise, it is easier to embrace a fitness regime when we are in a good place mentally.

Earlier in this chapter, we explored physical health using the acronym SPACE: sleep, presence, activity, creativity, and eating. I am writing this section in early January and the emphasis on physical health in social media, television, and newspapers is enormous. There is a pressure to repair the perceived damage done by the excesses of the Christmas period. I would suggest that this mindset emphasises guilt and underlines retrospective remediation rather than positive prevention. You are the expert in your own life, you know what your body needs and we can decide upon our own physical health regime.

The same issue seems to be at play in terms of our mental health – we don't value it until we have lost it. We live in a fast-paced world with a variety of daily pressures and stresses. Our mental health regime may not always rise to the conscious level. Raising awareness of your own mental health provides a helpful starting point. It is worth investing in creating the conditions that will enable you to thrive. It could be argued that we need to take responsibility in this process and design our personalised mental health regime. *What works for you?*

Spiritual health generally seems to occasion less emphasis than the physical and mental. Perhaps spiritual health is much harder to define and therefore we do not place as much emphasis upon it. How would you define spiritual health wealth? This may be a significant plank in your lifestyle or one that you choose to ignore. You are the expert in your own life. The relationship between mind, body and spirit is a fascinating one that merits attention and analysis. Starting from the premise that prevention is better than cure, please use the questions below to interrogate the state of your health wealth. Bank accounts work better when you have made more deposits than withdrawals!

Exercise 18 Health wealth

How would you define health wealth?

Audit your physical health – use SPACE or any other framework to support your review. You may enlist the help of professionals such as your GP, personal trainer, or other specialists.

Audit your mental health – what is your mental health regime? How do you invest in maintaining positive mental health?

Audit your spiritual health – start by defining what spiritual health means for you. Would you like to maintain, modify or radically change your current approach?

What does the mantra 'prevention is better than cure' mean for you in terms of the investments you are making in your own health wealth?

Feedback and reflection: an opportunity to grow

Feedback from trusted others is a useful mechanism in triangulating our self-awareness. It is often seen as binary – positive or negative. This is an over-simplification as feedback is often more nuanced than that. Out of choice, I prefer receiving positive feedback as it reinforces my self-esteem and the way I choose to see myself. Negative feedback may sting, nevertheless it can have a galvanising function and generate new thinking and ways of behaving. It may be helpful to differentiate negative feedback from developmental feedback. The criterion may be the intention of the provider.

Feedback is the seed corn of reflection. It enables you to see yourself clearly and it provides a starting point for self-review and future action. However, Eleanor Roosevelt provided a useful caveat to taking all feedback on board. I am re-wording her message: in essence she said, *I reserve the right to ignore feedback from people whose judgement I do not respect.* This is eminently sensible as sometimes feedback tells us more about the person providing it than the person receiving it. Having said that, it would be foolhardy and blinkered to ignore developmental feedback that becomes a launch pad to future success.

Evaluate feedback in terms of the insight and understanding of the person providing it. Your mastermind group and other people you trust are fertile starting points. Feedback may come formally in a work situation, or informally in a social setting. It may be verbal or non-verbal. Keep your reticular activating system (RAS) open to sieve the valuable information that is coming your way. Your reaction to feedback, in whatever form, provides a valuable starting point for reflection. Developmental feedback provides the basis of reflection as a growth activity.

The artist Claude Monet[34] put it succinctly when he suggested "It is on the strength of observation and reflection that one finds a way. So, we must dig and delve unceasingly." Reflection is not an indulgence it is a very effective way of learning from experience. The challenge is to find the time and space to do it successfully. How do you manage the process of reflecting? Do you snatch time in the shower or while driving, or do you set aside time to stop and think deeply? A quiet time, a planned meditation, or random thoughts on the run all have a potential part to play. You may have developed an eclectic approach. The key question is *Does it work?*

I want to sit back and think more. Coaching has made me more reflective!

Several interviewees indicated that answering my questions had caused them to think, reflect, and act. Reflection is the precursor to action. Indeed, coaching could be seen as focused reflection, as you hear what you are saying when you speak it out loud and you decide upon the action you plan to take. Structured reflection leading to reflexive action is a wonderful recipe for success. Skilful questioning deepens this process further. You may ask yourself the questions or work with a trusted other.

This book is designed to support your reflection on your past, your future and your NOW. As you look outwards and then turn the telescope to look inwards a range of lines of investigation will appear. Which ones are the most interesting and fruitful for you? I have designed the exercise below to provide an entry point to this reflection. You decide how you want to deepen and widen it.

Exercise 19 Feedback and reflection

Feedback and reflection could be seen as two sides of the same coin. I suggest you review the way you undertake both processes in your life.

Feedback

From whom do you get formal feedback?

From whom do you get informal feedback?

Whose feedback carries the most weight?

How do you manage the feedback you receive?

Reflection

What is the nature of your reflection strategies?

Would you like to modify them in any way?

Do you avail yourself of the support of others?

Identify the main themes emerging from the study of this book that you wish to reflect on further.

Postscript

The end is nigh – you have almost finished reading the book. In fact, I hope it is not the end but rather the beginning of your journey to living a conscious life-style: a life by design, not by default!

"Every action you take is a vote for the person you wish to become."[35] Take it one day at a time – inhabit the moment. I am not a big fan of massive change. Jumping from the bottom of the stairs to the top in one giant leap for mankind is not a sensible strategy unless you are a superhero! I have found taking one step at a time is a more effective approach. Your small daily choices will accumulate to shape the future you want.

You are the expert in your own life. You are the person best placed to decide the steps you wish to take. You know your current circumstances and what will work for you. Children are natural born learners, and we need to apply the same childlike confidence to learning in our adult lives. Take a risk and see what works for you. Give yourself the benefit of the doubt and be patient with yourself. Resist the discouragement of your inner critic and nurture positive self-talk.

Keep your inner mental chatter focussed on the positive. Become your biggest fan rather than your worst critic. Enjoy your life and devote yourself to becoming the best version of yourself. We are designed to be 'human beings' rather than 'human doings'. Establish a *to be list* to sit alongside your *to do list*.

Look back through your learning journal and celebrate the progress you have made. Review what you have gained from the exercises, the text, and the ideas of academics and researchers. Invest in some solid reflection time and draw your own conclusions. "Let the views of others educate and inform you, but let your decisions be a product of your own conclusions."[36] Use your conclusions as a springboard to the next step in living your own conscious lifestyle!

Bibliography

1. Reinhold Niebuhr – prayerfoundation.org, 2. Comer, J M (2019) The Ruthless Elimination of Hurry, 3. Tolle, E (1999) The Power of Now, 4. Sheehy, G (1984) Passages,5. Warren, S (2019) The Pain Relief Secret, 6. Peters, S (2011) The Chimp Paradox, 7. Rotella, R (2015) How Champions Think, 8. Silva, J (1978) The Silva Method, 9. Nestor, J (2020) Breath, 10. Hof, W (2022) The Wim Hof Method, 11. Billy Graham – azquotes.com, 12. Rohr, R (2018) Just This, 13. Skidelsky, R & Skidelsky, E (2012) How Much is Enough?, 14. Sasaki, F (2017) Goodbye Things, 15. Deborah James – indy100.com, 16. Chapman, G (1992) The Five Love Languages, 17. Esther Perel – growcounselling.com, 18. Thomas Monson – quotesvibes.com, 19. Henry Ford – goodreads.com, 20. Elvis Presley – awakenthegreatnesswithin.com, 21. Mahatma Gandhi - goodreads.com, 22. William Barclay – wow4u.com, 23. Sebastian Coe – azquotes.com, 24. Pink, D (2009) Drive, 25. Seligman, M (1990) Learned Optimism, 26. Ellen Langer – freshquotes.com, 27. Andrew Castle – Sunday Times 24-07-2022, 28. Grant, A (2021) Think Again, 29. Davies, S (2013) Laughology, 30. Brownlee, A (2021) Relentless, 31. Dyer, W (1990) You'll See It When You Believe It, 32. Obama, M (2018) Becoming, 33. Paul McGee – Twitter 01-01-2023, 34. Claude Monet – azquotes.com, 35. Clear, J (2018) Atomic Habits, 36. Jim Rohn – azquotes.com

LIVING A CONSCIOUS LIFESTYLE

Index

Printed in Great Britain
by Amazon